UN MOVING FOUR WARD

UN MOVING FOUR WARD

TALES + TIPS FOR KEEPING PERSPECTIVE DESPITE LIFE'S CHALLENGES

Bob Bell

NORTH STAR PRESS OF ST. CLOUD, INC.

St. Cloud, Minnesota

To the Juder

Table of Contents

Prologue

Ulaanbaater

IT'S POSSIBLE TO SMILE with a face full of Mongolian piss—or so I learned the hard way.

It's decidedly more difficult, however, to smile with pants full of the D-word. Oh, yes, the dreaded D-word. It's a word we're all very familiar with, yet we hate to say it. We universally cringe when we hear it. And we absolutely, positively, hate to have it.

It makes people run away faster than Lorena Bobbitt clutching her husband's favorite boxing partner. It makes them feel more stupid than former FEMA director, Mike Brown*ie*, sitting on a patio at Pat O'Brian's in New Orleans sipping a hurricane. And it makes everyone more uncomfortable than Sarah Palin and Snookie at a book fair.

It's really green and runny, but it's actually not that funny—even when sliding into home and your pants begin to foam.

It's *diarrhea*.

And when traveling in a foreign country, this better-left-unspoken word is often at the forefront of your mind. You're breathing, eating, and drinking a veritable concoction of bizarre germs. And sometimes, unfortunately, and unbeknownst to you, this concoction transforms you—hocus pocus—into a magician, performing the worst of all human magic tricks:

"Ladies and gentlemen, please watch and see with your very own eyes as I turn this perfectly good pair of ordinary pants into a perfectly horrific pair of greenish-brown corduroy pants."

For this very reason, Imodium pills are a staple of all experienced travelers. Like a good rain jacket or passport and money holder that goes under your shirt—these items are carried at all times.

Yet Imodium is just the starting point: Pepto-Bismol tablets. Tums. Tylenol. Aspirin. Alka-Seltzer. Hell, if you throw in a few blank postcards and a Slurpee machine, most veteran travelers could open their own 7-Eleven.

Keeping antibiotics close at hand is also a standard experienced-traveler move, the obtaining of which requires a pre-departure visit to your doctor. Cipro (500 milligram tablets) is a typical hook-up. Beg on bended-knee for a full bottle if you have to; anything to avoid finding yourself sick and stuck in a foreign country searching for a doctor, or heaven forbid, in a hospital—especially if you don't speak the native language.

It was our last night in China when I started taking Cipro.

"You look like shit," Jeff kindly informed me, the way only a good friend can.

It was the summer of 2005 and we'd already been traveling for close to two months. Jeff and I had been best friends since college, and we were sitting at a coffee shop in the Beijing airport, waiting for our flight to Ulaanbaatar, Mongolia. Germs from the previous eight countries were sloshing around inside of me.

By the time our plane touched down in Mongolia, my stomach had invented a loud language of its very own. We made our way through customs, grabbed our bags, and I headed for the bathroom.

It was in the Ulaanbaatar airport bathroom that I transformed into a combination of Davids: David Copperfield and David Blaine. And much to the amazement of my caregivers, I transformed the color of my pants in the blink of an eye—unfortunately, it was a brown eye.

The next forty-five minutes were about as humiliating, degrading, and disgusting as you can imagine. My caregivers picked me up out of my wheelchair and laid me on the cold linoleum bathroom floor. The bathroom was small, and my head ended up directly under a urinal. As my caregivers rolled me from side to side cleaning me up, Mongolian piss caked my face.

Jeff stood guard outside the bathroom door the whole time. I knew he wouldn't allow anyone in. Even when security showed up, Jeff didn't budge.

When I eventually emerged from the bathroom and saw Jeff's face, it was clear he had a sense of what I'd just been forced to endure. Men sometimes don't communicate as well as women, but Jeff's expression said all that needed to be said. He was very concerned and utterly empathetic.

"How ya feeling?" he asked.

"I've had better days," I woefully retorted, full of melodrama, sarcasm, and self-pity. I regretted my response instantly as it just hung there.

Within an instant, my mind rolled back to that cold November night when my neck was broken, and then to a lifetime of events that followed. I'd already spent fifteen years in a wheelchair by the time I exited the bathroom in Ulaanbaatar, and there'd been plenty of good days and plenty of bad days since then. I just needed a moment to put it in perspective.

After a flash of reflection, the dust began to settle and the situation fell into its proper place. "But I've had worse days, too," I added lightly, with a smirk forming and a twinkle in my eye.

"Let's catch a cab and give this town some hell!" I finally said, smiling widely, with a face full of Mongolian piss.

AND THAT'S WHAT THIS BOOK is really about: understanding that you *will* have good days, you *will* have bad days, and you're not alone in your struggles. Perspective like this allows you to realize the bad days aren't as bad as they seem, and there are plenty of good days around the corner.

If you think you're the only one to ever endure a breakup, a divorce, a death, an illness, an injury, an addiction, a crappy job, a lost job, or whichever one of life's many challenges you're facing right now, well, then you've lost perspective.

Look around. Open your eyes. It could always be worse. And guess what? It pretty much always gets better. So focus on the positive. Start making plans for some fun. Get to working on achieving whatever goals you want.

In the end, when all is said and done, if you choose to face your challenges head-on, you'll come out on the other side proud of yourself, which is what matters most. But here's the kicker: as a truly magnificent bonus for accepting your challenges with courage and grace, those who love you will love you all the more. I promise you that.

So enjoy the ride. Every rollercoaster has its ups and downs. Just be glad you're not stuck upside down on the Ferris wheel . . . with a dire case of the D-word.

Chapter One

Collegeville

ONE OF MY HIGH SCHOOL TEACHER'S husband's friends had gone there. My connection to Saint John's University was that strong.

The summer before my senior year in high school, my mom and I drove twenty-two hours from Pensacola, Florida, to Collegeville, Minnesota. The drive took us three days. And by saying "my mom and I drove," I mean *she* drove. I slept most of the way.

Her station wagon had one of those bench seats in the front. You know, where the passenger is forced to sit as close to the dashboard as the driver.

A woman named *Judith* at birth, predictably nicknamed *Judy* thereafter, and due to lots of lovable and laughable idiosyncrasies (as well as many monumental acts of motherhood) my mother is now known to most simply and affectionately as *the Juder*.

She stands barely five feet three inches tall, is so skinny she needs to hold her breath to cast a shadow, and can damn near rest her chin on the dashboard when driving.

At close to six feet tall, my knees were next to my ears when riding shotgun with her—so backseat bound I became.

Not long after we hit the highway, the oil light lit up.

"I checked da ole yesderdee," said the Juder (her accent part sweet southern debutante drawl, part Richard Petty at a Budweiser bass fishing tournament), "an' it wuz fhine."

With her head under the hood at the first roadside gas station, she kept pulling out the dipstick, wiping it, guiding it back in, pulling it back out, and studying it. "Look like need'tad lease 'nother quart."

A single mother since I was four and my sister was six, she learned to do a lot for herself. More than she ever expected to, undoubtedly. More than she ever wanted to, most certainly. But her independence made her proud. That lesson by itself made one of the biggest differences in my life.

Not back on the road very long, the oil light came on again.

"Sorry, dear heart" she said, "but we're gonna haft turn off da air. Sometin' wrong witda car."

It was early August, hot and humid. The windows in the backseat were childproofed and didn't roll down. The upholstery, a baby-puke yellowish-beige, was made of a plastic so cheap it was less like pleather and more like Tupperware—it absorbed my sweat like a formica countertop. And undulating overhead, through the sagging bubbles of roof-fabric, was a dense, whitish-gray oxygen-sucking cloud: remnants of an exhaling Juder, a three-pack-a-day smoker.

It was her idea to make this trip. We'd already visited several other colleges over the past year. But the annoyingly consistent advice from everyone and their mother was to apply to several colleges: the long-shot, the sure-thing, the back-up, the in-state, the out-of-state, the one-just-to-shut-your-parents-up, and more.

It seemed the only people *not* giving advice on applying to college were . . . well, there weren't any. *Everyone* felt like the string in their back had been pulled.

Of the schools we had visited thus far, most were located in the south: Clemson and Furman in South Carolina, Auburn and Hunting-don in Alabama. I visited Florida State with some friends—a school neither encouraged nor discouraged by my father, an alumnus (he started at Sewanee, but dropped out because his parents couldn't afford it), or by my mom, a student at FSU for two years before she dropped out to marry my dad and cook meals for him while he went to law school at the University of Florida (a time of different choices for women; a time fortunately behind us).

On our drive up to Saint John's, I also interviewed at Saint Thomas University in St. Paul, Minnesota. At the time I didn't know any more about Saint John's than I did about Saint Thomas. During my interview there, however, I learned that only about 1,000 of the 10,000 Saint

Thomas students lived on campus. As a Florida boy destined to live in dorms, once I learned this fact I didn't consider Saint Thomas any further. Only later did I learn that Saint Thomas (where the students are known as *Tommies*) and Saint John's (known as *Johnnies*) are fierce rivals. Looking back on it, although I'd yet to possess the proper vernacular to describe it then, my interview at Saint Thomas was my first exposure to one of the few constants in life: *Tommies Suck!*

After my interview, it was back to the backseat for me as we drove for a little over an hour from St. Paul to Collegeville. And once again, I slept most of the way.

To this day, the Juder and I laugh about how much I slept on that trip. We didn't think it was really strange at the time that I was sleeping so much. I was a teenager, after all, and I'd just had my wisdom teeth removed a few days before we left. In retrospect, however, maybe we should've been tipped off that something was amiss by the fact that the back of her car was so covered in oil we couldn't see a damn thing through the back window. For a total of forty-four hours of driving, I was stuck in the backseat without any ventilation. Not only was I desperately trying to swallow a gulp of fresh air through the fog of the Juder's chain smoking, but we were leaking oil like the *Exxon Valdez* tanker. By the time we returned to Pensacola, we'd gone through twenty-two quarts of oil.

I wasn't sleeping back there, I was freakin' asphyxiating!

THE FIRST THING I SAW when arriving on campus at Saint John's is the first thing everyone sees: a massive and imposing church bell banner.

A structure standing 112 feet high and 100 feet across, the bell banner is surprisingly both masculine in size and composition and chic in design. The brainchild of famed architect Marcel Breuer, it reflects the strength, individuality, and ruggedness of an all-men's college located on a wooded campus in the middle of Central Minnesota. Yet in the flip of a switch, if it were moved next to the MoMA in Manhattan, even the most discerning and highfalutin' art aficionado, sipping Merlot and stroking the elbow patches on his black turtleneck, couldn't help but give it two snaps and a twist.

Its shape is basically that of an upside-down trapezoid (if you're a geometry geek) propped up by four curved legs. (Also described as "vertically cantilevered," but who the hell knows what that means?)

Centered at the top of the inverted trapezoid is a large cutout space in the shape of a rectangle turned on its side. Inside the space, carved from one of the many white oaks found on campus, is a wooden cross.

As you drive to campus after exiting Interstate 94, it's this space, and this cross, where your eyes naturally settle. It provides a simple choice: you can allow your eyes to focus on the emptiness surrounding the cross, or you can focus on the cross itself. It's up to you. Life is about where you choose to focus.

Lined up below this are five huge brass bells, balanced symmetrically—ascending and then descending in size—with the largest bell in the middle and each weighing in at over four tons.

The bell banner is backdropped by the Abbey church, a structure every bit as unique and hip, the front of which consists of almost nothing but colorful honeycomb-shaped stained glass windows.

They say the honeycomb shape is the strongest shape nature has ever produced. Its strength is the result of each of its sides working with the honeycomb next to it, so that no single honeycomb bears the full weight alone. By working together, the combined honeycombs are able to bear a tremendous amount of weight, much more than they could ever bear individually.

The bell banner and Abbey church are simply a sight to behold, which unfortunately was equally true (albeit for totally different reasons) of the embarrassing eco-disaster of a station wagon that had just pulled into a parking space below it.

As the Juder turned off the ignition, we both just sat for a moment in silence, pleased with ourselves for finally reaching our destination. Everything looked just the way a college campus should: regal brick buildings, storied ivy cascading from the walls, and luscious green grass. (Oh, yes, this was Minnesota well before the winter!)

And off in the distance, making his way slowly toward us—on his way to the church—was a monk in full habit. His black robe extended to his feet and the fabric looked coarse, like burlap. (Star Wars dorks can envision a Jawa wearing black. Or imagine a ninja in a robe with a hoodie—but a very austere ninja, if not a bit pious.)

The plan was for me to interview with someone in the admissions department, and then stroll around the campus to check it out. After seeing the monk, however, my mind was pretty much made up.

"I could never go here," I said to the Juder. "I'd be kicked out in a second."

Unfortunately, I wasn't kidding.

It's certainly not that I was the worst kid in the world, it's just that I wasn't always the best kid either: held back by the Juder in second grade, a regular cigarette smoker by third grade, arrested in front of my class for burglary and vandalism in fourth grade, and started drinking alcohol by eighth grade. Throughout all of grade school and high school, the Juder was subjected to countless conferences and phone calls with teachers and principals for her boy fighting, misbehaving and receiving terrible grades. As my sweet, skinny, church-going granny used to say, "We pray for C's for Bob."

No, I wasn't the worst, but much further from the best. And my mom, bless her heart, knew it all too well.

I'm sure she secretely hoped Saint John's could turn me around. If only she knew how that would happen, I doubt she would have ever let me out of the car.

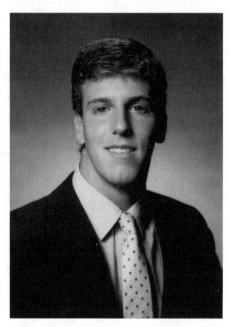

THE WORDS "COMMUNITY" and "Benedictine hospitality" are thrown around in Collegeville so often that sometimes they bring a smile. Yet when you experience them firsthand, you know they're true. And in the admissions department at Saint John's, I was blown away by how genuinely nice and welcoming everyone was to me. I'd heard about the concept of

High school senior year photo. (Oh, to have hair again.)

"Minnesota nice" (the stereotype that everyone is friendly in Minnesota), but these people in admissions were serious as hell about being nice.

On the other hand, I was completely clueless as to what I was getting myself into. I'd never seen snow or owned a real jacket or pair of gloves in my whole life. It sort of "snowed" a couple of times while growing up in Pensacola, and we literally put sweat socks on our hands to play in it.

I remember as a senior in high school scraping the windshield of a car with my sweat socks, trying pathetically to build up enough of this white stuff for a snowball. A friend of mine beat me to it and tagged me with his snowball. As the sting began to set in, I thought to myself, *Those kids up north must be pretty tough. These snowballs freakin' hurt!*

Little did I know that our "snowballs" were basically "iceballs," and didn't resemble in the slightest real, soft, fluffy snow.

I interviewed with a woman who didn't seem much older than me. She was a relatively recent graduate of the College of Saint Benedict, the sister school to Saint John's. Saint Ben's is an all-women's college of about 2,000 students, the same as Saint John's is an all-men's college of about 2,000 students. (Saint John's also has a graduate school in theology which admits men and women.) Buses shuttle Johnnies and Bennies the four miles between campuses almost every fifteen minutes until late at night. Students attend classes together and share a joint academic program. It's basically one school with two campuses. Saint Ben's and Saint John's are as much a part of each other as each state is a part of the United States: they each retain their own identity, but they make up one country. And the community among them is not unlike a colorful honeycomb.

At the time, however, I didn't know anything about Saint Ben's, and the Juder and I didn't drive the extra five minutes over to St. Joseph to go check it out. I just knew this woman I was interviewing with was gorgeous and figured if there were a few more like her still at Saint Ben's, then it would be totally fine with me.

Following the interview, I walked around Saint John's campus a little bit with a student from the Bahamas, but then it was time to get back on the road.

As we headed to the car for our return home, I looked at the Juder and said simply and matter-of-factly, "This is where I'm going to school."

It was the only school I applied to.

Chapter Two

Collegeville 2.0

FAST-FORWARD TO THE END of this story and it plays out like an ABC After-School Special. I'm lying on a hospital table in the emergency room with a whole team of doctors and nurses hovering over me. Large bright white lights are beaming down on me from every angle. My shoes, T-shirt, sweatpants, and underwear were just cut off my body with scissors.

I'd hardly ever been to see a doctor in my whole life, but if you've watched enough after-school TV, you know the question you're supposed to ask.

I heard my neck crack three separate times when it happened. I couldn't move then, and I'm afraid to try to move now. I'm lying there, naked, in front of a bunch of strangers. But there are bigger issues that need to be addressed.

Everyone takes a deep breath. (A commercial break must be coming up.) I look up at the doctor who appears to be in charge and ask the question that feels too dramatic and extremely over-rehearsed.

It's a five-word question with an answer that will impact every day of the rest of my life, although I had no idea what that life would be like.

But I follow the script and ask the question.

"Will I ever walk again?"

There's a long pause before his response. (Of course there is.) It felt like everyone in the room was looking at me before, but now they are all *really* looking at me—looking into my eyes to see how I'll respond to his answer.

They already know the answer. They've seen this episode many times before (and seen my x-rays). For them, the question and answer are reruns—it's how I respond to the answer which transforms this into excellent reality TV for their viewing pleasure.

I search their eyes for hope. I'm hoping to see hope. *Please, someone, smirk or crack a smile.* My question was so damn corny, wasn't it?

But no such luck. Instead, the neurosurgeon gave me the cold hard truth. It took me a few seconds to understand his answer. (In truth, it took me a few years to understand.) But it's been true every second since the words passed over his lips.

The funny thing is, the corny question I felt required to ask was not the one I wanted to ask. I was thinking about something totally different. My question had nothing to do with long walks on the beach. My question was exactly what every nineteen-year-old boy thinks about constantly—well before walking.

Will I ever have sex again?

TUESDAY, NOVEMBER 21, 1989, was two days before Thanksgiving during my freshman year at Saint Ben's/Saint John's. I woke up around 6:30 a.m. because I wanted to shower and eat breakfast before going to court in the nearby city of St. Cloud. I'd been arrested for using a fake I.D about a month earlier. There was initial talk of charging me with burglary. When they caught me I was trying to open the dorm window of a girl I was sort of dating at Saint Ben's. The problem, unfortunately, was that I was so drunk I had the wrong window. When the officer asked for my I.D., I opened my wallet and he *saw* my fake I.D. and took it. I was therefore heading to court to dispute the charges. After all, I never said it was me—at least not *that* night.

I told myself when I started at CSB/SJU that I was going to turn over a new leaf. Not a single, solitary person in the whole school knew who I was. I could be whoever I wanted to be. No one would be calling me to head out and party, or think it strange if I didn't. And if I didn't want girls to be a distraction for me, that was my choice. My plan was to study hard and get good grades.

Since school started, however, I'd not only been arrested for a fake I.D., but I'd also been caught with alcohol on campus a few times, completed more than my share of "work hours" for being caught with girls in my dorm room late at night, and was becoming somewhat infamous with the nuns at Saint Ben's for the brash and novel ways I was able to sneak into the girls' dorms. (Save for the night I was arrested.)

Father Cletus, dean of students at the time, had recently written a letter to the Juder detailing some of the infractions her wonderful son had committed to date. He was also gracious enough to provide me with a copy of the letter, which I promptly photocopied and sent to all my friends in Florida, as well as framed and displayed prominently on my dorm room wall.

Father Cletus also informed me in no uncertain terms that the next time I was caught for anything—absolutely *anything*—he was kicking me out. "You need to start looking for a school down south," he portended, much to my devastation.

By all accounts, it seemed as though my epiphany upon seeing a monk during my first visit to campus was becoming inevitable.

A buddy of mine, Todd, who lived across the hall from me, knew today was my court date. He told me the night before he wanted to go with me so that I wasn't alone in the courtroom. He also knew they were predicting snow, and offered to drive me since I'd never driven in snow.

It was one of those offers from a friend that makes you realize just how good a friend they are—or, more accurately, just how good a person they are, and how lucky you are to have them as a friend.

Most of my friends thought I was an idiot to fight the charges. They were convinced I'd get myself into further trouble by going to court. But I gave my court-appointed attorney a favorable rendition of the facts, he pleaded my case to the judge, and I got off with twenty-five dollars in court costs and nothing on my record as long as I didn't get arrested again during the next six months.

We made it back to campus in time for most of our classes and in plenty of time for me to gloat about and embellish my courtroom triumph. It was beautiful. Every person at school who heard about it thought I was the luckiest man alive. And my reputation for being able to get myself out of anything was bolstered significantly. You see, with as many things as I'd been caught for, I'd gotten away with a whole lot more.

Around six o'clock that evening, I made time for a workout at the gym—focusing only on lifting weights with my legs.

I jogged back to my dorm in a beautiful, light snowfall that made me appreciate for the first time the quiet and serenity that accompanies a snowfall at night. I ran up the four flights of stairs to my dorm room, but decided to stop by Todd's room first. I

Move-in day, freshman year at CSB/SJU. (One of my last pictures standing.)

knew he wasn't there, so I could use his phone with some privacy. (Alas, the days before cell phones.) I called the Juder in Pensacola to recount for her my successful day in court, and to give her the contact information of the friends I'd be staying with during the Thanksgiving break.

After the call, I opened the door to walk across the hallway to my room. What happened next is something I've relived in my mind millions of times.

Standing in front of my door was the boy who lived in the room next to mine. I had a sweatshirt draped over my shoulder, and upon seeing him standing there, I tossed it at him and said something in a rude tone, like, "You're blocking my door, man."

Those actions changed the course of my entire life.

I HAD DECIDED A FEW WEEKS earlier I didn't want to wrestle with this boy. Like typical testosterone-filled guys, we had been wrestling around one day when he picked up one of my legs and started pushing me backwards, forcing me to backpedal on the other leg. By the time I lost my balance, I fell mostly onto someone's bed. I remember thinking that if I hadn't been such a world class athlete (exaggeration) and the bed hadn't been there to cushion my fall, I would've fallen on the cement floor and likely been really hurt. So I told myself to stay away from this kid.

The two of us were more acquaintances than friends. We'd been living next to each other for the last three months, but that didn't mean we knew each other. He was a freshman starter on the football team and a muscular guy. I was fairly muscular as well, so there was undoubtedly some sort of alpha-dog mentality going on. And, yes, there was the small fact that I'd spent the night with his roommate's "ex-girlfriend" the first weekend of college. But I'm not entirely sure he was aware of that. (I know his roommate wasn't!)

So when he lunged at me after I threw my sweatshirt, I just sort of stood there and did nothing, thinking he would realize I didn't want to wrestle with him. This made it easy for him to quickly spin me around, thread his arms under my armpits, clasp his hands around the back of my neck, and begin pushing down. It's called a "Full Nelson" wrestling hold. Almost every male I've ever met has been in one. And it's technically an illegal hold in wrestling—for a good reason.

When I started to feel pain in the back of my neck, I tried to push my head up. At that point, however, I didn't have any leverage. My neck was already bent too far forward.

Several other students were in the hallway watching as it happened, including one of my best friends, Omar. The moment between throwing my sweatshirt until falling to the floor seemed like an eternity. But it all happened in a matter of seconds. Three separate and distinct "pops" were buried within those precious few seconds, and then one life ended and another began.

The first pop was likely no more than a simple cracking of the neck. It sounded like, and probably was no different from, when someone cracks their neck or knuckles. But it certainly felt different at the hands of someone else. Nowadays when people crack their neck to relieve tension, it sends chills up my spine—a figure of speech full of irony in my case.

Omar was standing no less than four feet away from me before the second pop happened. He saw the contorted angle of my neck and undoubtedly saw the fear in my eyes. He screamed out, "Let him go. You're gonna break his fucking neck!"

His words echoed in my mind for years after that day. *Was there time to stop? Why did he keep pushing? Why didn't he stop?*

Omar and I have never spoken about his plea to this boy, but I hope he doesn't feel like there's something more he could have done. It all happened too fast. There was nothing anyone could have done. But when Omar yelled out, I tried one last time to push back. It was too late.

The second pop is likely when the bone broke. It was much louder than the first pop, and it took my breath away. But I was still standing. My arms were still outstretched. My hands were still reaching upward. Yet he kept pushing.

And then the third pop rang out. It followed the second much quicker than the second followed the first. It's likely there were only a matter of milliseconds between them, but I can still hear the difference like it was yesterday.

None of the pops caused me any intense pain. And the third pop actually hurt the least, which is when I believe my spinal cord was damaged—when the broken vertebrae from the second pop was forced into my spinal cord.

They say the spinal cord is like an electrical highway. It has electrical currents constantly running up and down from the brain to the tailbone, distributing messages throughout the body. The spinal *cord* is protected by the spinal *column*, which are those bones (vertebrae) you see protruding down the back of emaciated runway models.

Starting at the base of the skull, the spinal column consists of seven cervical vertebrae, twelve thoracic vertebrae, five lumbar vertebrae, and then the sacrum and coccyx (the butt-bone and tailbone). The degree of seriousness of a spinal cord injury is based on where in the spinal cord the injury occurs. Breaking the neck and injuring the spinal cord at the first cervical vertebra—the vertebra closest to the skull—results in death. It's that simple.

If someone is injured at the second cervical vertebra—where Superman, Christopher Reeves, was injured—they'll live, but will mostly only be able to blink their eyes, chew food and swallow, and move their head slightly. They're otherwise paralyzed from the neck down and can't even breathe on their own. They need a machine (a ventilator) to breathe for them for the rest of their lives. Or, with the help of modern technology, they may be able to breathe without a ventilator during the day with the aid of electrical stimulus, which is where doctors attach electrodes to the diaphragm and force it to contract, thus enabling the person to breathe without a ventilator. It doesn't work as well at night, though, so they're still stuck on ventilators while they sleep. (All of this will hopefully improve with time.)

In JoJo Moyes's book *Me Before You*, the main character, Will, is said to have been injured between the fifth and sixth cervical vertebra (a C5/C6 quadriplegic), although his motor function more closely resembled someone injured at the third cervical vertebra and cannot move their arms to feed themselves.

Progressing down the spinal column, the degree of injury becomes less catastrophic, though still profoundly devastating in its own right. For example, an injury to any of the cervical vertebrae is worse than an injury to any of the lumbar vertebrae. But try blowing this sunny piece of knowledge up the fanny of a paraplegic who was just told they will never walk again.

The reason an injury to the spinal cord is so complicated, and often so devoid of hope, is because the inside of a spinal cord looks like the inside of a telephone line, with millions and millions of tiny wires—way too many wires to try to figure out which one connects with which. (And yes, I know I just lost a few whippersnappers who only know of satellite, but they'll have to trust me on this.) Yet even if doctors could figure out how to connect the wires, the worst problem with an injury to the spinal cord is that it's made up of tissue that doesn't regenerate once it's damaged. Unlike a scrape to an elbow or knee, once the tissue of the spinal cord is damaged, it's damaged for *good*—which ain't so *good* at all.

THE THIRD POP WAS DEFINITELY the loudest of the three, but not so loud as to be deafening. Yet once it happened, everything went completely quiet.

I watched my legs curl up underneath me and saw my arms drop down. It was as if the puppet master dropped the strings to his marionette.

I imagine it took a second or two for him to feel the full weight of my body in his arms, and that the feeling of my body transforming into dead weight must have been startling. Either way, he knew the pushing was over. He loosened his hold and my lifeless body began its descent toward the concrete floor—the same floor I feared hitting a few weeks earlier.

I remember thinking as I fell, *This is really gonna hurt.* But when I landed, it didn't hurt at all. In fact, I didn't feel a thing. Little did I know, I *couldn't* feel a thing.

My left elbow hit first and absorbed most of the impact, and this helped to roll me onto my back. How my head avoided hitting the concrete, I have no idea. But there I was, lying on my back in the hallway of my freshman-year dormitory, looking up at the boy who had just changed my life.

The first words out of my mouth came to me from my days as a Boy Scout. I'm an Eagle Scout, a fact that the Juder would make sure you know. It's a goal she ferociously pushed me to achieve, and one which provided me one of my first tastes of the sweetness of achieving a significant goal—although the badge really should have been given to her.

In Scouts, you learn that when someone receives a neck or back injury, you should try not to move them at all; you could end up actually causing a spinal cord injury, or exacerbating one that has already occurred.

"No one touch me," I said as loud as I could. "This is serious."

I knew my neck was broken. And I knew I had a spinal cord injury. I just had no earthly idea what that really meant.

My next words were common sense; we learn them almost from birth. It's quite surreal, however, when the words come out of your own mouth and you realize just how much you mean it, and then you much you really need it.

"Someone call 911."

18

It was indeed another ABC After-School moment.

The final words out of my mouth were all I could think of as I looked up at the boy who had just broken my neck.

I was nineteen years old. I was as immature, self-absorbed, and caustic as the worst-of-the-worst of anyone at my age. So what I said to him then caught even me by surprise. It was unquestionably a figurative step, but as I reflect back on my life in a wheelchair, I know it was my first step to recovery.

Looking up at him, I said his name, and then spoke clearly:

"I know that was an accident. I forgive you."

Tip #1
Life Will Have Challenges

FIND THE PERSON who told you "Life is going to be fair," and then kick 'em in the fucking teeth. Because guess what? They lied to you!

"Why me?" is the question asked time immemorial by almost everyone who has ever faced one of life's challenges. But how often do we ask "Why *not* me?"

Why not you? Why isn't this *your* time to face one of life's challenges? Why someone else, but not you? And what made you believe you would have no challenges in life in the first place? Did someone tell you that? If so, they lied to you!

Understanding that life *will* have challenges, and that you can't pick and choose which ones you want, is critical in learning to accept your challenge and in overcoming it.

Life absolutely, positively, most definitely *will* have challenges. You should expect it. Plan on it. Bank on it. Don't act like it couldn't happen to your sweet ass.

So when one of life's challenges comes along—and it *will*—just accept that this is your challenge. Or add it to the list with your other challenges. But accept it either way.

The sooner you come to terms with the fact that this is your challenge, the sooner you can decide *how* you're going to deal with it. And that's when you start making progress. That's when you start moving forward.

Chapter Three

St. Cloud

T AKE YOUR PLACES, EVERYONE! The commercial break is almost over. It's time for Bob's response to the neurosurgeon.

The camera naturally zooms in for a close-up of my eyes.

"Will I ever walk again?" was the question I'd asked him before the commercial break (feeling cheesier than the cheesiest of soap opera actors.)

Dr. Watts had a reputation for his lack of bedside manner. He told it like it was. No sugar coating. No pussyfooting around.

With his impressive full head of white hair, he looked every bit the part. Yet when he walked, he had a slight limp, and one of his eyes seemed to droop a bit. Only later did I learn he was a polio survivor. Having spent years walking in braces and in rehabilitation, pity wasn't an emotion Dr. Watts exhibited readily.

"Son, you're a quadriplegic," he told me directly.

A what? I thought. *What'd you say? What the hell is a quadriplegic?*

I'd asked him if he knew whether I'd walk again. I had no idea if quadriplegics walked. Actually, let's forget this walking crap. I wanted to know if I'd have sex again.

Seriously, dude, what the fuck is a quadriplegic? Can I get laid or not?

My mind swam in a torrent of thoughts. In the screenshot of my eyes they lost any semblance of solace—exactly what the director wanted.

The word *quadriplegic* meant nothing to me. I'd heard the word *paraplegic* before, but I really had no idea what it meant, either. I'd seen wheelchair basketball players on TV, and those wheelchair dudes at races with huge, muscular arms. I started to piece together that *para* of *para*plegic probably meant *two*—as in *two legs* injured, although not their arms. Those guys could definitely still move their arms.

But what was the difference between *para* and *quad*? If *para* means *two*, does *quad* mean *four*? I remembered hearing that somewhere before.

And it hit me just like that. And (oh, Nellie!) the director must have been thrilled with the look in my eyes. We're talking Emmy award-worthy TV.

Because it was right then, for the first time, that I tried to move. And I mean, tried to move *at all*—not just my legs, but my arms, too. I tried moving all *four*.

You see, it wasn't only that I asked for no one in the hallway to touch me, but I didn't even try to move myself. I was afraid I'd further injure myself by moving.

But now, when I tried as hard as I could to move my legs (*para*) or my arms and my legs (*quad*), nothing moved. I could barely lift my head from the table, and that was it. Nothing else moved.

I'm a quadriplegic ran through my mind for the first time.

ALTHOUGH INCOMPREHENSIBLE CHANGES had occurred in my life during the last few hours, the date somehow remained the same. It was still two days before Thanksgiving.

The original plan was to spend the Thanksgiving weekend at two different friends' houses, both of whom lived in Iowa. Going home to Pensacola for Thanksgiving was too far away and too expensive for such a short vacation.

For most people who go off to college, returning home has a sort of fantasy allure to it. You think about how great it's going to be to see your family and friends again. You feel you've changed after moving out of your parents' house. You grew up. You became more adult. You've experienced new things, and look forward to returning as a bit of a different person. And if you also happen to have a high school girlfriend or boyfriend waiting for you when you return, it makes it all the more exciting.

Lying there paralyzed, I wasn't immune to such fantasies. I'd already journeyed far down this road when thinking about my return to

Pensacola for Christmas break, even going so far as knowing exactly what I'd wear on my second plane ride ever. I'd imagined it so many times that the look on my high school girlfriend's face when she saw me at the airport was almost as though it had already happened.

So under the watchful eyes of a room full of people, I found myself suddenly switching my Christmas break fantasy to Thanksgiving break (leaving out, of course, the little part about now being paralyzed).

Will I be able to fly home soon to recuperate from this pesky little injury? Will it be within the next few days?

It seemed unlikely. But maybe.

And so, to break the silence from Dr. Watts telling me I was now a quadriplegic, I wondered out loud to everyone in the room, naïve as it was. "Well, I guess I won't be going home for Thanksgiving," I said to no on in particular, secretly hoping it might somehow not be true.

But Dr. Watts didn't (or couldn't) break from character, his brutal honesty uncontainable.

"Son, you'll be lucky if you go home for Christmas."

And just like that, the bottom dropped out of my world. I lost all equilibrium. Any sense of direction escaped me. All concept of time vanished. I was lost beyond lost. My eyes slowly closed.

Who stays in the hospital that long? I thought. *I was planning on going home for Christmas,* I pleaded to no one but myself. *What the hell do you mean "lucky" if I'm home by Christmas? I'm going home for Christmas, you son-of-a-bitch!*

The only response I could muster was a fallback on humor and sarcasm—two things that have always come to me naturally, whether I wanted them to or not. And two things that aren't *always* one and the same, which I learned way too late in life.

In this case, however, using humor and sarcasm was much better than breaking down in front of total strangers.

I'd asked the dramatic question, gotten the harsh answer, and now I had to choose the ending. It was an ending for them, at least. It was just the beginning for me.

I looked into the eyes of those around me and forced a tiny grin.

"Merry Christmas, everyone," I half-whispered.

I don't think the director liked it.

THE JUDER ARRIVED AT ST. CLOUD HOSPITAL slightly before noon the next day. She hadn't slept a wink the night before and caught the first flight from Pensacola to Minneapolis.

She gave strict orders that no one be allowed in to see me before she arrived and was able to see me first. Tasked with being my nurse for the next twelve hours, Greg wasn't looking to cross this pushy woman with a southern accent. So even though they'd been waiting for hours, Greg wouldn't allow any of my friends from the overflowing waiting room in to see me—including the boy who broke my neck, who was waiting with the rest of them.

It is of course every parent's worst nightmare to receive a call like my mother did.

"Your son has been in a wrestling accident. He's now a quadriplegic," Dr. Watts explained over the phone to my mom.

"A what?" said the Juder.

"A quadriplegic."

"Can ya spell dat fo' me?"

Later that night, the Juder called an emergency room in Pensacola and asked a doctor whether a newly injured quadriplegic would likely survive through the night or die. This doctor not only took the time to assure my mom I should survive, but also explained to her the surprisingly fulfilling and spectacular life I should be able to live, despite being a quadriplegic.

Buoyed somewhat by his optimism, she admitted she doubted whether his prognosis could ever prove true. Her next agonizing hours were spent packing, traveling, and wondering what her son would look like as a quadriplegic.

When she walked into my room in the intensive care unit, the Juder found me lying on my back, hands at my sides, with a metal contraption screwed into my skull (traction). Undoubtedly anticipating some sort of dramatic and emotional reunion with her now-quadriplegic son, what she received instead was more typical of a teenager.

"Hey, Mom," I said nonchalantly, "Good to see you. Thanks for coming so fast. Listen, my friends have been in the waiting room all morning. Is it okay if they come in now?"

24

We still laugh about that introduction to my quadriplegic-domness, or whatever the hell you call it. It appears the script writers at ABC After-School Special were on strike.

Not to disappoint, however, I quickly created some dramatics. I knew the boy who broke my neck had been waiting all morning to see me. I asked my mom to let him in first.

Greg and I had talked for hours about how I felt about this.

"He meant to hurt me," I told Greg. "I have no doubt about that. You don't put that kind of pressure on the back of someone's neck without the intention of causing some pain. He was trying to prove he's stronger than me, and that I shouldn't mess with him anymore. But I truly believe he had no intention of hurting me like this."

Lying on my back in the dorm hallway, I had seen the fear in his eyes. The breath taken away from me after the second pop had been taken away from him as he watched me crash to the floor. And to a certain extent, I'd been him before: the boy who played a bit too rough and unintentionally hurt somebody. Forgiving him as I did seemed clear at that time.

Greg listened to me, but he wasn't sure it was a good idea for me to see him so soon.

"I understand your concern, Greg," I continued. "But I'm okay with seeing him. He hasn't been sitting down the hall waiting all morning because he wants to come in here and laugh at me or say 'I told you so,' or to finish me off, for God's sake. He's sorry. He feels bad. He meant to hurt me, but he didn't mean to do this."

Now, with the Juder finally here, I told both Greg and my mom that I was comfortable with my decision: I wanted to see him first.

Greg left my room to go get him, and the Juder stood by the door. It seemed like an eternity before they returned, but when Greg finally walked back in my room, there was the boy who broke my neck.

Despite whatever mixed feelings the Juder most certainly must have felt about coming face-to-face with the boy who only hours earlier damaged her son's life forever, he was crying so badly that she couldn't help but give him a hug.

Greg walked around the bed and leaned down to whisper in my ear, "Would you like me to stay?"

"No, you and Mom please step out of the room for a few minutes."

With that, I was alone with the boy who broke my neck.

Slowly, he walked over and stood beside my bed, placing his hands on the hospital bed guardrail. He looked at me right in the eyes, but he couldn't stop crying.

"I'm sorry. I'm sorry. I'm so sorry," he repeated over and over.

I listened to him for a while without saying a word. It was important to me to hear what he said. I believed in my heart that what happened was an accident, but suddenly, with him standing beside me, I really needed to hear it from him—not necessarily in the words he chose, but in how he said it . . . how he looked when he said it.

But after hearing him and seeing him, I felt a strong sense of finality to our conversation. I realized we should never have this conversation again.

I'll admit a little Hollywood sappiness took over me (coupled with an ample supply of painkillers), so what I said next started off a bit scripted and dramatic.

"What?" I said. "I can't hear you."

He repeated, and repeated, and re-repeated, how sorry he was.

"What?" I said, "Come closer. I can't hear you."

Again, his tears flowed and his sorrow poured out.

"Please, lean down and speak louder so I can hear you."

He began again.

This last time, however, I hardly listened. I mostly just watched and waited for him to finish. I wanted everything to be perfectly clear.

I have no idea where what I said next came from, or why saying it felt so evident. I've replayed it in my mind so many times that I believe what I've written below are the exact words I used:

"I want you to know I've listened to every word you've said. And I've heard you say you're sorry over and over. What I said to you yesterday in the hallway, I'll say again now: 'I forgive you.' I don't believe you meant to hurt me like this. So now I'm going to ask you to promise me one thing. Please do this for me. Promise me that you'll never apologize to me again. You and I both need to move on from this. And there's no reason for you to keep apologizing. It was an accident, and I forgive you. Promise me you won't apologize again."

And with that, our conversation pretty much ended.

Over two decades have passed since I spoke those words to him, and I've told this story hundreds of times. Yet I never cease to marvel at whatever grace or maturity passed over me in that moment. I remain today as utterly proud of what I said, and of the sincerity with which I meant it, as I was the second after I spoke to him.

I certainly have no way of knowing how my life would be different if I chose to harbor resentment or hatred for this boy, or even if I chose to blame myself for what happened. What I know for sure is that letting go of this has made my frame of mind much clearer and my outlook much more positive. Avoiding being weighed down by such negativity has proven to be very cathartic in the coping process. And Lord knows, coping with a serious challenge in life is difficult enough without expending negative energy on the blame-game.

There's no undoing the past. But for each today and for every tomorrow we're fortunate enough to be given, we're provided with an opportunity to choose how we want to live our lives. We're all given this choice. And I truly believe my choice has freed me to have the amazing life I've had so far, and to be the person I am.

To THIS DAY, THE BOY who broke my neck has kept his promise: he never apologized again. And while I've seen him many times since that emotional day at my bedside, it's been close to twenty years since I last saw him.

People often ask me if he and I ever became friends. My response is that we were never friends before the accident; we were different types of people. Forcing a friendship based on an event we both wish never happened makes no sense. But he has always been very respectful when he sees me. Several times we've been together in large crowds, in loud places. And when I spoke, I could tell he was providing me his undivided attention. That may seem trivial, but it mattered to me.

I suspect for him, however, that being around me is difficult: a harsh reminder of something he'd rather forget. That said, a few years ago I heard through a mutual friend that one of the things he's doing with his life is to be a caregiver for a quadriplegic—a man with an injury just like mine.

What a wonderful choice.

Tip #2
It's Not Just About You

CHRISTMAS DAY THE JUDER walked into my room in the ICU at St. Cloud Hospital and announced herself with a cheery, "Mherr Christmas, dear heart." She then kissed my forehead and proceeded to turn on the lights of the tiny fake Christmas tree nestled on the shelf among countless "Get Well Soon" cards, random stuffed animals, wilting flowers, and deflating balloons.

Next, she pulled from a plastic bag a pair of colorful hackneyed Christmas socks, and giddily slid them onto my feet over the white stockings covering my legs to prevent blood clots. And as if that wasn't enough, she then revealed a standard issue Santa's hat, which she carefully placed on my head.

It was clear she was quite pleased with herself, and she stepped back to admire her work and chuckle, her droll little mouth drawn up like a bow. (If not for being so damn skinny, her belly would have shook like a bowl full of jelly.)

I was having none of it.

I'd now been in the ICU for thirty-five days. I'd been told I was paralyzed for the rest of my life. And I was clinging to life by a ventilator.

About a week after my accident, I stopped being able to breathe on my own and almost died the night it happened. At first they couldn't figure out why I wasn't breathing. They intubated me, performed two angiograms on my heart (thinking it was a blood clot), and ultimately realized my left lung had collapsed and my right lung was filled with pneumonia.

Throughout that night, I felt like I was paddling a canoe on a river and was nearing a waterfall. I was paddling upstream to avoid going over the waterfall, but after hours of doing this, I was completely exhausted. I didn't think I could paddle anymore. I told myself I couldn't paddle anymore. I didn't know what would happen if I went over the waterfall, but I knew it was drastic. So each time I felt that I was nearing the waterfall, I'd fight once more. I'd paddle as hard as I could. And then I'd tell myself I couldn't do it again. *The next time, I'm gonna go over the waterfall,* I'd tell myself.

I'm too tired to do it again. And when the next time came, I'd somehow find the strength to fight again. And so it went from 7:00 p.m. until 3:00 a.m., when they finally stabilized me.

It took five people to hold me down during much of the night, even though I was only able to move my head and partially move my arms. My mom and a nurse held down one arm, my dad and another nurse held down the other, and nurses took turns holding my head—each of them trying desperately to keep me from damaging my neck further. They pumped sixty-five milligrams of valium in me and had my mom sign something acknowledging that I may die from some of the procedures they were doing. All the while they asked my parents to keep an eye on my legs. "If he's still able to move his legs, it will likely show tonight," they said.

There was no movement.

So here I was on Christmas Day, still in the hospital, just like Dr. Watts said I would be. And I was at my lowest point of this whole saga.

It all started five days earlier, December 20, which marked the day I originally planned to fly home from college. The Juder had purchased the ticket for me months before, and as I mentioned earlier, I'd spent an inordinate amount of time fantasizing about my return home.

Despite all the dramatic medical events and emotional discussions I'd had with people since my neck was broken, it was only when the nurse wrote "December 20" on the whiteboard next to my hospital bed that a full dose of the reality of my situation finally took effect. I went into a tailspin, basically becoming inconsolable and totally depressed.

As Christmas Day began, I had no intentions of breaking this trend—certainly not to participate in anything that resembled the Christmas spirit the Juder was trying to push on me. My spirit was gone. It departed on a December 20 flight to Pensacola that left me behind.

Seeing all this, my mom stopped her charade. She stood quietly for a moment next to my bed and looked at me. What she said next helped me realize something very important—something I've never forgotten as I've faced challenges in my life.

"Listen, Bob," she began, "Lotta people gone ta lotta effort ta make taday a special day fo' ya. If tomorra ya wanna go back to feelin' sorry fo' yourself and bein' all sad, well fhine. But taday, ya will smile, say thank ya, an' be appreciative fo' everythang everyone done fo' ya."

Damn, I thought. *That stings.*

This was not what I wanted to hear. And despite feeling like I knew this little woman redolent of smoke pretty well, it was not what I expected her to say. Within a few minutes of being forced to swallow that bad medicine, however, I knew she was right. And for the first time since my accident happened, I realized that what had happened to me hadn't *only* happened to me. There were a lot of people around me who loved and cared for me who were hurting, too. It wasn't just me. It was just that I was only thinking of me.

The Juder's tough love helped me then, and it's helped me as I've faced many other challenges since that Christmas day.

Keep that in mind as you face whatever challenge life is throwing your way. There are people around you who love you and are sharing your pain. They need you just as much as you need them. And you should support them just as much as you hope they'll support you.

Smile. Say thank you. Be appreciative. Be supportive.

Because even when spending Christmas on a ventilator, it's not just about you.

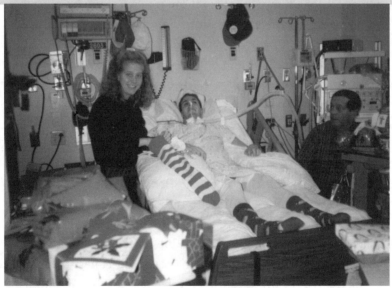

Christmas day on a ventilator, with my sister and dad.

Chapter Four

St. Louis

IT WAS COLDER THAN FROSTY'S icicle with shrinkage when the doors opened at St. Cloud Hospital. The closest thing to cold, fresh air I'd felt since late November was when the ventilator would pop off of my tracheostomy and blow cool air in my face. All sorts of bells and whistles would sound and nurses would come running. It was frightening at times, but often I was burning up so badly with a high fever that trading cool air on my face for life-saving breath in my lungs seemed like a fair trade.

I'd been able to breathe without the ventilator for less than two weeks when we left the hospital for the airport. An air-tight patch covered the open hole in my throat from the tracheotomy. And much to my embarrassment, I was wearing adult diapers to cover my, uh, um . . . other open holes.

Smothered in blankets and flat on my back, they rolled me out on a hospital gurney through the same doors I'd entered two months earlier. I could instantly see my breath backdropped against an electric blue sky and beaming white sun—shocking to eyes atrophied from months of fluorescent lights. With the ambulance waiting only a few feet away, the cold air strangely felt hot for an instant.

It was certainly not the return to Pensacola of my pre-paralyzed dreams, but I was finally heading home!

My early departure from St. Cloud Hospital was possible because I was insured through Blue Cross and Blue Shield *of Florida*. They were tired of paying Minnesota rates (which they couldn't negotiate), so a deal was struck that I'd return to Florida if they paid for the air-ambulance—

a $25,000 expense they were willing to pony up to get me back on their turf.

At takeoff there were four of us in a small Learjet that essentially functioned as a flying ambulance. It was me, the Juder, a nurse, and the pilot. The nurse was a nice guy in his early forties, sporting some serious Farrah Fawcett feathered hair. He said he'd worked as an air-ambulance nurse for many years.

With my head beside a window as we ascended into the clouds, I said goodbye to Minnesota—possibly forever. We flew for an hour or so and then the pilot said we were landing in St. Louis, Missouri, because we needed to refuel. To this day, I have no idea if this refueling was planned or if a problem created our need, but when we landed in St. Louis on a cold and rainy January morning, I saw the Gateway Arch in the distance. I now think of this day every time I see the Arch.

The plane taxied over to an area where we were able to get fuel. Before I knew it, we were gassed-up, back on the tarmac, and taxiing toward takeoff. As we started to gain speed down the runway, however, I began to notice from the corner of my eye some sort of vehicle moving up alongside us. Even with our engines roaring, I thought I also heard the faint sound of a honking horn. I strained to turn my head toward the window, and with that a dark pickup came fully within my view. The driver was frantically waving his left arm out the window, desperately trying to get our attention. I understood I lacked a fair bit of flying experience, yet I still surmised this probably wasn't the way airports say goodbye to people who buy gas from them. So I yelled to everyone that something might be wrong.

As it turned out, we were gushing fuel from our plane, and the guy in the pickup saw it and came racing after us.

They immediately shut down our gas-soaked plane and had it towed to a safe area for fixing. That's when things got interesting.

Our plane was now on the ground where it was raining and the temperature hovered just above freezing. We weren't able to turn on the heat because that required turning on the plane, which was spewing fuel. And did I mention I was wearing a diaper? Yeah, well, it was now wet.

People with spinal cord injuries—especially those newly injured— have a difficult time regulating their body temperature. They're like women in their fifties, but also with cold flashes, and without vaginal dryness. So it didn't take long for our situation in the plane to go from uncomfortable to dangerous. My whole body began to shake. Something needed to be done.

They determined it would take too long to fix this plane, so they radioed for another air-ambulance to fly to St. Louis and take us the rest of the way. That was the good news. The bad news was that it would be four or five hours before that plane could arrive. By then I'd need an air-hearse rather than an air-ambulance.

So, some calls were made and the next thing I knew I was being transferred into a heated ambulance parked on the tarmac, which is where I resided until the next plane arrived.

All the while, the Juder was frequently leaving me and going into the airport where she said she was calling my grandmother and father to keep them apprised of when we might arrive home. Each time she returned, however, she seemed more and more distressed. I thought it was just because of our current predicament. But as the hours passed and she went to make phone call after phone call, she eventually came back to the ambulance with tears in her eyes. She sat down beside me and sighed.

"I'm sorry," she began, "but dare wuz a surprise bein' planned fo' ya dats now nolonga gonna happen. Dare wuz gonna be lots a people at da airport in Pensacola to greetcha. Sister Kirsten (my high school principal) planned to let da boys 'n' girls varsity an' junior varsity basketball teams outta school to meetcha at da airport. Day even arrange fo' a fire truck ta be dare. But now, cuz da delay, mosta people not gonna be able da be dare. I'm sorry."

At nineteen years old, this was crushing—especially when seeing the pain in my mother's eyes. There would be no crowd of friends to welcome me home. No fire trucks. No parade.

It feels like God isn't really looking out for me, I thought quietly.

Within several hours, the second air-ambulance arrived and we were again airborne. I was uncomfortable, hungry, and soiled. This day had gone on too long. But despite everything, I still couldn't help but be excited. I knew Nicole, my high school girlfriend, would be at the airport waiting for me, and I couldn't wait to see her.

"We're beginning our descent into Pensacola now," the nurse told me a few hours later. "We should be on the ground in twenty minutes."

Little did I know how long those twenty minutes would stretch on, or how much they would impact me.

My family and friends who were able to wait at the airport in Pensacola said it was the weirdest thing they'd ever seen. It was a perfectly clear night, and then, out of nowhere, they could barely see ten feet in front of their faces. Fog as thick as peanut butter stuck to everything.

We'd begun our descent and the landing gear was down. But the pilot and nurse were talking feverishly back and forth. Then, all of a sudden, we began to climb quickly.

"There's way too much fog down there right now," said the nurse. "You can't see a thing. We're gonna circle around and give it a few minutes to clear out."

Over the next hour, we tried several times to land, but it was too dangerous. Eventually we were running low on fuel.

"We're gonna try one time," said the nurse, relaying the pilot's plan to the Juder and me. "But if there's too much fog, we're gonna fly to the Mobile, Alabama, airport and try landing there."

I couldn't believe my ears. *What the fuck? I'm not going home tonight? I'm not seeing my family and friends tonight? I'm not seeing Nicole tonight?*

The entire time I'd been in the hospital, I hadn't questioned my faith in God once. Not once since the minute I hit the floor did I question whether God was with me. Oh, yes, I'd prayed to Him with unbridled intensity for my paralysis to go away. Prayers so pointed and persistent they could bore holes into diamonds. Most of the time, I wasn't even greedy; I prayed endlessly just to be able to move my fingers. I'd forgo walking if only I could have full use of my hands. And even though my paralysis remained virtually unchanged through all these prayers, my faith in God never wavered. Until now.

As we descended for our final attempt, I began a conversation with God. I told Him I knew what I was about to do was wrong, but I couldn't help it. I was at the end of my rope. I'd never questioned Him before, and I promised I'd never do it again. I wasn't saying that I definitely wouldn't believe in Him, I just told Him that I'd find it to be very difficult.

And so I made my ultimatum: *Allow us to land, or I will question my faith. But I promise to never do this again.*

It's a story I don't tell readily and haven't told often. I'm embarrassed by it, mostly because it demonstrates weakness in my faith. (And of course the juvenile nature of an ultimatum to God makes me look like a pretty big asshole.) But I also don't like to tell this story because I don't want anyone to think it's okay to do what I did, or that I *think* it's okay to do what I did, or that others can try it sometime to get what they want (read: don't try this at the blackjack table in Vegas).

My family and friends on the ground said that just as inexplicably as the fog appeared from nowhere, it disappeared as soon as my plane touched down on the tarmac in Pensacola.

It still troubles me, however, to think about how my life would be different if we hadn't landed in Pensacola. I'd like to believe I would have returned to my faith, even if I'd lost it for a while. Because I can't imagine how much harder it would be to handle my injury if I felt like I was alone.

For any atheists or agnostics reading this and facing one of life's challenges, my message for you is simple: Fuck you! Burn in hell, motherfuckers!

(Okay, I'm only kidding.)

I actually really feel for you. I mean that sincerely. Not because I want to try to convert you. You can believe or disbelieve whatever you want. I'm not a Bible-waving, verse-shouting, crew cut-sporting, pasty-white boy, standing in the hot sun on a busy street corner, wearing black pants, a white short-sleeve button-up shirt, and a cheesy 1980s black skinny-tie. (If you've ever been condemned to hell by one of these little bastards in the Bible Belt, trust me, you find baby Jesus in a hurry praying for that red light to turn green.) But that's not me.

I'm simply letting you know what you're passing up. And I'm certainly not advocating any specific religion. I was born and raised Catholic, but I recognize the Catholic Church has more than their share of issues. Hell, its handling of child molesters by itself leaves it without basis to judge others, not no mention its antiquated and delusional views of women, contraception, and whether priests should marry. (And let's not even get into the fixation many religions, states, businesses, and politicians have on determining which gender can morally assert a predilection for throat-yogurt and stink-wrinkles.)

Yet I remain Catholic today despite this. Resolved to be an agent for change within rather than merely a critic from without. Besides, let's call it like it is: our new pope, Pope Francis, is kicking some serious Papal ass right now. For the first time since I can remember, Catholicism has the wind at its back.

Then again, Judaism has one of the most fascinating histories of any religion, and wearing a yarmulke would cover up my bald head. I'd definitely consider joining that tribe, if it weren't that they can't eat shellfish. (This Gulf Coast boy is convinced God loves shrimp and fresh crabmeat with melted butter sauce.) Similarly, I've traveled in Lebanon and seen some of the most beautiful women in the world. I'd sign up to be a Muslim in a minute if it weren't that I already have enough problems dealing with airline security. (And the list goes on.)

The point I'm pathetically trying to make is that a strong belief in God has made it much easier for me to deal with my injury and with other significant challenges I've faced in my life. It helps that I believe God exists and watches over me. I believe God is present in my life. I believe I'm not alone in any significant trials or tribulations I face.

I remember back in 1999 when Jesse "The Body" Ventura was governor of Minnesota (a time many Minnesotans may wish to forget) and he did an interview with *Playboy* magazine that was quite controversial. While reading the magazine for its excellent articles, I came across Jesse's interview (excuse the pun) where he says, "Organized religion is a sham and a crutch for weak-minded people who need strength in numbers."

My knee-jerk reaction to his quote was that it only confirmed my suspicion that there may be a few flaws in electing people to higher office who wear feathered boas and jump off the top rope to *fake* pile-drivers on their colleagues. I mean, no self-respecting postal worker worth his or her weight in mental illness would ever *fake* hurting a colleague like that.

But the more I thought about Jesse's use of the word *crutch*, the more I liked it. And certainly a guy like him who has hurt himself so many times jumping off the top rope must know a few things about using crutches.

Think about what a crutch is. It's something you use when you're hurt. Something you lean on and supports you. Something that gives you strength when you're not at your strongest. You could probably go without it, but you wouldn't heal as fast, or maybe you wouldn't heal at all.

It's certainly one way to think about faith in God. And when you're facing one of life's challenges, it may prove helpful. At the same time, it's important to balance the comfort provided by that crutch with being sincerely thankful for all there is to be thankful for. (And the fact you're reading these words—or hearing them or touching them—leads me to believe you have plenty to be thankful for.) It can be illuminating (and disheartening) to recognize how infrequently we pray "thank you" prayers versus how often we pray "I want" prayers.

In this vein, over the last several years, I've grown to take the words "Thy will be done" from The Lord's Prayer much more literally.

"*Thy will be done* on earth, as it is in heaven."

Who am I to judge what God's will is for me while I'm on earth? Is it really some sort of negotiation where I can change His mind? Or could it be that His will is just for me to try to do the best I can with the life I've been given? I don't know. But I like the way that sounds. And someday maybe I will know. Until then, I'm just glad He's with me. Trying to do this alone would suck.

WHEN WE DISEMBARKED the plane in Pensacola, the nurse looked like he'd seen a ghost. He had been with the pilot in the cockpit as we landed. All he could do now was shake his head from side to side.

"I have no idea how the pilot landed this plane," he finally said. "I was right there beside him, and I never saw a thing."

Chapter Five

Pensacola

A S MUCH AS I HATED leaving my friends in Minnesota, it was great to be home. Save for cheap plastic beads and stale moon pies, my hospital room in Pensacola was a veritable Mardi Gras parade of family and friends constantly stopping by each day: my dad, my stepmom, my best friend, Adam—they were the Grand Marshals, ushering in a colorful, eclectic, and oftentimes awkward tapestry of friends and relatives. For fun, we developed a one-to-ten scale to gauge how uncomfortable my visitors were to witness a real-life quadriplegic. (Or, as was often the case, to gauge how uncomfortable they made me feel.)

The Juder, of course, was there every day, too. But she arrived late in the evening—always with a fresh load of laundry. She'd returned to her job as a customer service representative at First Union Bank. Having received two months of paid time off, she felt she needed to return right away to show her appreciation.

And most important to me, Nicole was there every single day. She never missed a day. Just as soon as she got out of school each day, and every weekend, all weekend long, she was there.

It didn't take long to settle into some sort of weird rehab hospital routine, and I felt like I was adjusting well. West Florida Rehabilitation Center followed the typical protocol of any spinal cord injury rehabilitation hospital: they assign you a doctor, an occupational therapist, a physical therapist, a recreational therapist, a primary nurse, and my least favorite: a psychologist.

I don't mean to disparage the whole psychology profession, but every psychologist I came across during my time in hospitals seemed infinitely more damaged than anyone else. On the day I left West Florida Rehab, for example, my psychologist completely lost it on me. She told me, among other things, that I was "the asshole of the whole world." And while I'm not necessarily denying this may, in fact, be the case, it's just I'm thinking, for professional reasons, she might have wanted to keep that to herself.

Despite my lack of progress with my character flaws while at West Florida Rehab, I made tremendous progress there physically, especially considering that I arrived on a gurney, flat on my back. Before long I was sitting up in a wheelchair, learning how to feed myself, how to write, and how to push a wheelchair. I started lifting small weights to gain strength, and I was eagerly looking forward to getting out—so I could get Nicole naked again.

In many ways, however, my time at West Florida Rehab was quite difficult for me. I was the only spinal cord injury patient there. I spent my days surrounded by elderly stroke patients and volatile head injury victims. I had no role models. I had no idea what the road ahead of me might look like or how high or low I should aim. The only person I knew in a wheelchair was the atrophied boy staring back at me in the mirror. And I barely recognized him.

Ironically, one of the greatest things I learned at West Florida Rehab had nothing to do with any formal rehabilitation regimen. One morning as a nurse began helping me, I was lying in bed completely naked, with no sheet covering me. Just then, three other nurses walked into the room and began having a conversation at the foot of my bed. These nurses were fully aware of my state of dress, they just chose to disregard it. Truth be told, after spending close to three months in hospitals, this didn't faze me in the slightest. I'd lost all sense of modesty, dignity, and pride. I didn't really even see myself as a human being anymore.

I'm sure it sounds strange to hear of someone think of themselves as anything other than human. But if you've ever experienced a significant stay in a hospital, you know what I mean. There's unfortunately no shortage of doctors and nurses who see patients in much the same way a car mechanic sees a car: as an object they've been hired to fix.

I don't doubt that dealing with patient after patient, day after day, year after year, could desensitize almost anyone to certain aspects of caring for people. But that doesn't change the way you feel when *you're the patient*. To you, being in the hospital is likely one of the biggest events in your life, and you are at your most vulnerable ever. To you, you're different from all the other patients. After all, this is *you*, goddamnit!

Suddenly, one of the nurses realized the situation and grabbed a sheet to cover me up. As she brought the sheet up from my feet and over my chest, she leaned down and whispered in my ear. The other nurses were still chatting away, oblivious of their actions.

"No one can take away your dignity unless you give it away," she whispered.

It's amazing how one statement—sometimes one word—can completely change your entire perspective. (Think of how a simple yes or no to the right or wrong question can change forever how you feel about someone.) There I was, lying naked on the bed like a cold, dead cadaver at the morgue, feeling like a piece of meat in the worst possible way. I'd long passed having any feelings of humiliation. Instead, a pathetic sense of apathy and indifference were all I could muster. Sadly, I'd allowed the desensitized way many people viewed me to dictate how *I* viewed myself. My paralysis had without question caused me to lose a great deal of control over how my body worked, but I'd forgotten I still retained 100 percent control over how my body would be treated.

And so with the whispered words of this nurse, I went from powerless to empowered in an instant. Having lost so much control over the last several months, I grabbed hold with both hands to the precious amount I still very much possessed. It felt freakin' awesome!

AFTER THREE MONTHS OF REHABILITATION at West Florida Rehab, it was time for me to leave. As my discharge date approached, I recall preparing myself for what I felt would be a dramatic conversation with the Juder. I needed to ask if she could really handle me moving home and taking care of me. In my mind, I was willing to move into a nursing home if that's how it needed to be. I knew it would be hard. I knew I didn't want to go into a nursing home. But I didn't want to be a burden on anyone.

But the Juder never considered anything other than her boy coming home. My dramatic conversation with her lasted about twenty seconds. She learned how to take care of me, and I was soon back at home.

My change of venue from hospital to home, however, did nothing to dwindle the parade of visitors—they kept marching on. Other than when I slept, I was never alone. The Juder would get me up in the morning before she went to work, my stepmom would then come over for a few hours, my grandmother would relieve her at lunch, Adam would help me into bed for a nap, Nicole would come over after school, my dad would stop by after work, and then my mom would be home from work.

My life consisted of a lot of motion but lacked any sense of direction. I accomplished virtually nothing each day. It was all repetition.

The Juder was pushing me to finish up a few of my classes that Saint Ben's/Saint John's was allowing me to complete via correspondence, but even that was a constant battle between us. I didn't want to do anything—not that I really even had a clue what I should be doing. I was at home, but I was basically still a patient in the hospital. In fact, the Juder was waking up at night to turn me every two hours when I slept. She barely slept at all.

Not surprisingly for a boy my age, the only area of my life where I still had focus was my relationship with my girlfriend. Nicole and I had been dating for a little over three years, and our time together at West Florida Rehab had brought us much closer together while simultaneously pushing us apart.

She was eighteen years old, on the brink of graduating from high school, jaw-droppingly gorgeous, and constantly being pursued by a cavalry of slimy swains. Prior to my injury, our relationship was largely based on sex. This is not to say that we didn't go through all the motions and emotions of having a complete relationship—dates, dinners, dances, discussions, disagreements, delight, and disappointment—it's just that when you're that young, it's hard to attach much depth to it.

What my injury allowed me to see, however, was just how much Nicole really did care for me. Her devotion to me while at West Florida

Rehab left me astounded. Almost from the start, I suggested we break off our relationship, recognizing it could never be the same again. I gave her every out possible, and even tried to pretend like I'd be the one to end it. But there she was again the next day.

At one point, due to an adverse reaction from medication, my entire face broke out into the most disgusting cornucopia of pimples ever seen. Nicole sat by my bedside and popped those zits with nothing but affection in her eyes. It's gross, but it's a great memory for me. To feel love like that is extraordinary.

Not long after I moved back home, she and I were finally alone one afternoon. There was only one thing on my mind.

"Lock the front door," I told her. "Let's try having sex."

I was nervous as hell. Prior to my injury, the two of used to bury the baby leg like it was going out of business. Yet this was entirely different. In rehab, the basic sex therapy they provided was simply that everyone's body is different. As a man, they essentially said that if the forest is still able to grow some timber, you just need to ask your partner to climb the tree and see what happens. It may fall down. It might ooze some sap.

What a difference a year makes. At prom with Nicole my senior year of high school, and at her senior prom a year later.

Nicole transferred me to the bed, and we thus commenced our crash course in dendrology.

Before advancing too far, however, we heard the front door open.

"I thought you locked the door," I growled through gritted teeth.

"I did!" Nicole implored, jumping up from the bed naked.

Grabbed her shorts and darting to the back bathroom, she left me in bed alone. Lying there with my pants down around my ankles and a towel covering my lumber yard, I tried my best to look innocent when into the room walked Adam, who was followed by Brian, our soon-to-be architect, who was followed by . . . *my grandmother*!

(Lord have mercy!)

Brian was there to explore options for building a new bedroom on the back of the house. My old bedroom—where I slept before my injury—was up a few stairs in our small house. With that room no longer being accessible, my post-injury bedroom was a makeshift setup in our main floor family room, which is why it was so easy for them to walk in and find me.

I'd never met Brian before, but he was quick on his feet when he entered the room, saw an empty wheelchair parked next to the bed, and found me in the supine position with knobby knees exposed and a lace bra beside my head. He promptly diverted my grandmother to the kitchen and jumped back into the room to toss the bra behind the bed.

Still attempting to do his job (or at least feigning to do so for my granny's sake), he decided to check the back bathroom for possible ways to tie it into my new bedroom. Upon opening the door, however, he found Nicole, sitting on the toilet, with her hands covering her bare chest.

"I think I've seen all I need to see," Brian loudly announced to my grandmother. "We can go now."

I only wish I could've been a fly on the wall when he got home from work that day. "And how was your day at work today, honey?"

I'm sure it made for interesting dinner conversation.

FOLLOWING MASS AT ST. MICHAEL'S Church in Pensacola, the Juder and I were in the parking lot struggling to transfer me back into the car. While at West Florida Rehab, I'd learned how to use a sliding board to transfer from my wheelchair to a car, but the way I learned, it still required the help of two people (or one really strong person). Nicole promised she would meet us at church to help, but she never showed up.

The first time after my injury that a friend took me out to a party, we tried to be a little creative with the transfer into his car. Michael was strong, stood about six-foot-three, and weighed well over two bills. We decided he'd put my legs in first. Then, while standing in front of me, he'd reach under my armpits, pick up my torso, and pivot me into the car.

In rehab they harped on the importance of "wheelie bars," but I hadn't really given them much thought. Wheelie bars consist of two pieces of metal that turn down from the back of the wheelchair. They usually have small wheels at the end of them, and their purpose is to keep you from flipping backwards.

My wheelie bars were turned up instead of down when Michael reached for my ankles to swing my legs into the car. The Juder was standing a few feet behind me, emotionally watching her boy resume his life and head out for the evening with a friend. But as Michael began pivoting my legs, they suddenly straightened due to a muscle spasm and my wheelchair started flipping backwards. The Juder lunged for the wheelchair to catch it from flipping, but she was too far away.

Feeling myself quickly tipping, I leaned forward to try to offset it— making it all much worse when the chair flipped over and my head snapped back against the concrete street.

Bam!

After seeing metaphorical stars, I laid there on my back looking up at the night sky, wondering just how badly I was hurt.

"I think I'm okay," I said after a moment. "Go ahead and set me up."

The Juder yelled to my sister, Karen, to bring a flashlight. It was dark and the Juder wanted to examine the back of my head.

"Well," said Judith, diagnosing my head injury with flashlight in hand, "ya bleedin'."

And with that, I was out. I passed out, or went into a seizure, or fainted, or something. I felt like I was underwater. I could see the Juder and Michael standing in front of me, blurry and refracted. I could make out that they were yelling at me. But I couldn't hear them or yell back through the liquid. They told me later that my arms were extended and shaking. But to me, it felt like I was simply fighting to make it to the surface, desperate for some air.

It lasted only a minute or two, and then I regained consciousness. Suddenly I could hear my mom yelling to Karen to call 911.

"No. Don't call 911," I gasped, bizarrely thinking mostly of the cost of an ambulance ride. As my head cleared, I don't know why, but I could tell this was not an emergency. I certainly felt very strange, but not like I needed to be rushed to the hospital. So I sat there for a second. (One solitary second, segueing into a pregnant pause.) And then it happened. The oft-repeated metaphor ultimately rang true: it knocked the shit out of me. I completely lost control of my bowels.

"Let's go back inside," I yelped abruptly as my stomach emptied all over me.

Once inside, Michael went upstairs with Karen and cried his eyes out. While I was unconscious, Michael was certain he killed me. Now he was left wondering just how severely he hurt me.

The Juder rolled me back to the family room/my bedroom, where we surveyed the situation.

"If ya don't go out wit'em tonight, he may never take ya out again," the Juder stated simply. "An' da rest ya friends will be scared ta take ya out, too."

I imagine this is not the advice most mothers would give their quadriplegic child sitting in their own feces, having just split their head open. But looking back on my life, I believe it's exactly this type of "get back on the horse" advice that has allowed me to suck it up when need be, and to persevere.

It took over an hour to clean me up and get me back in my chair. But when Michael came downstairs, I didn't say a word to him about what happened to me medically. Instead we simply went out and acted like the college kids we were: we got drunk. In retrospect, I realize how absolutely stupid of me that was, since I probably had a concussion. But Michael remains a great friend of mine to this day, and we laugh about that night every time we see each other.

Back in St. Michael's Church parking lot, the Juder and I hoped my transfer to the car wouldn't end with me bleeding . . . or excreting anything else. But it was obvious we were struggling to make it. Just then, Ed Chadbourne, a family friend and parishioner at St. Michael's, saw us and offered the assistance of his grandson. With his help, I transferred into the car safely, and we were on our way home.

Mr. Chadbourne's act of kindness was noble and helpful, and could have easily ended right there. Yet as is the case with any act of kindness, the question then becomes: Is there more I could do?

Throughout life we all consider the limits to which we can give. (Or rather, we *should* all consider the limits to which we can give.) The questions of "should I help? How can I help? Could I do more?" are the types of questions that ultimately change lives.

I didn't know it at the time, but Mr. Chadbourne was a multimillionaire. He made his money in the construction business and was acquainted with Alana and Harold Shepherd through various business transactions. In 1973, sixteen years before my accident, the Shepherds' son, James, suffered a spinal cord injury in a surfing accident in Brazil. The Shepherds subsequently formed a premier spinal cord rehabilitation hospital in Atlanta, Georgia.

Returning home from church, Mr. Chadbourne told his wife, Ruth, "We need to do something to help Bob Bell." He then called the Shepherds and changed my life.

The next thing I knew, I was heading to Atlanta to be a patient at Shepherd Spinal Center. I was beside myself with excitement.

Ironically, missing Nicole wasn't something I worried about in the least. She'd broken up with me shortly before her graduation and was now dating some needle-dick who pursued her even while I was in the hospital. Unfortunately, however, each encounter I'd had with her since then was beyond embarrassing. Not simply because she broke up with me. But worse, my wrecked emotions had manifested physiologically: I now literally became sick to my stomach whenever I saw her or talked to her on the phone.

Some things you can bluff. But it's hard to act cool and tough, and like you don't care, when you're leaning over your wheelchair blowing chunks.

I couldn't get to Atlanta fast enough.

Tip #3
Life Is Short—Make the Most of It

THE FEW TIMES I'VE BEEN asked to be a peer counselor for a newly injured spinal cord injury patient, I've invariably shared this tip with them.

It always starts out the same way: we're in the hospital and they're explaining how angry they are. They blame themselves, or someone else, or the unfairness of life. They're clearly depressed. And they're desperately searching for reasons to explain why this happened to them.

It's obvious they don't want to feel this way. And they feel guilty for being stuck in this state of mind. They want out, but they're locked in a cycle of feeling these negative feelings, followed by feeling guilty about feeling that way.

"The next time you're going through this," I eventually tell them, "allow yourself to fully live into it. Don't stop yourself. And don't feel guilty about exploring this."

It's only natural for anyone in a situation like this to hate what's happened, to look for blame, and to ask, "Why me?" (I know I did much of the same at their stage and later.) What's worse is that this misguided process is often exacerbated by people telling you things like, "There's a reason for everything." Or my personal favorite, that "God never gives us more than He knows we can handle."

What? God gave this to me on purpose? Because He thinks I'm a badass and can handle it?

I can just see God up there in heaven holding a bunch of cards which have life's challenges on them. He has a monthly quota of these challenges He has to dole out. Saint Peter is beside Him, giving Him advice.

"Hey, God," says Peter, "Have you looked at your cards lately? You've still got to get rid of three bankruptcies, seven divorces, forty-five cancers, and two flesh-eating diseases—all before next Tuesday."

"Yeah, yeah, Peter, I haven't forgotten. They don't call me God for nothing, dumbass."

"Well, have you considered Terrance for one of the cancers? I mean, I think he can handle it. He goes to church every Sunday."

48

"Are you freakin' kidding me? Terrance? He stubbed his toe on a sprinkler two summers ago while wearing flip flops and damn near became an atheist. That guy is such a Medamn ninny."

"Okay, good point. But how about Betty? She's a strong person."

"Yeah, you're right," God agrees. "And she loves the hell out of Me. Remember how well she handled that thyroid issue we gave her a few years ago? Holy shit, was she fat! And she never questioned Me once. For sure let's give her breast cancer. She'll rock that with her strong faith. But we're gonna have to switch it to inoperable brain cancer if Ricky dies in that BASE jumping accident. What an idiot that guy is! It will make for an awesome YouTube video, though. Ain't that right, Petey? Give me some skin, Hen."

No, for some reason I don't think that's how it works upstairs.

Instead, when I'm counseling a person, I ask that before they begin to really dwell on who or what is to blame for their situation, or before they begin to ponder "Why me?" they need to look at the time first.

"Just look at a clock and take note of what time it is before you begin," I say.

And then by the powers invested in by the State of Shangri-La, I grant them full permission to explore their profound questions.

"When you're done," I say to them next, "and I mean after you feel like you've *really* spent enough time thinking about these questions—I mean *really*—then take a look at the clock again and note how much time has passed. And then ask yourself what has changed. Ask yourself how things are different from the time you began until the time you ended."

And with that, I pause for a second to let my uneducated advice settle in.

"Oh, but I've got a little spoiler alert for you," I then add casually. "Guess what? Not a freakin' thing will have changed. It was a complete waste of your time."

Boom!

Of course, I do this with a smile on my face and a chuckle in my voice. I try to be very careful not to minimize their very real pain, or to fail to recognize that we all need space to heal. The timing for hearing any tough love like this needs to be right. Personally, though, I know I wasted too much time pondering questions that have no answers before I began to move on. And my aim is to help others avoid my mistakes. (Then again, the advice I give may be Exhibit A as to why I've only been asked to be a peer counselor a few times.)

BIZARRE AS IT MAY SOUND, I believe my ability to handle my injury—both in the early days and today—has been helped by knowing so many people who died much too young.

Alana Woods. Chris Williams. David Simmons. Tim Sanchez. Junior Villanueva. Ashley Donovan. Tommy Winn. Frankie Lovett. Chris Agnew. Ted Potthoff. Chili. Gary Powell. Katy Reeves. Tory DiNitto. Kate Hunt.

I think of these people often and talk to them during difficult days. I carry each of them with me always. And in so many instances over the years, they've carried me.

Each of them would love to have just one more day of life. Their lives all ended much too soon. For me to spend time complaining about my challenges, or to waste time placing blame, or trying to determine some mystical reason why this happened to me is to completely disregard the tragedy of their lives. These people lost everything. So to the extent possible—as best I can—I strive to honor them by making the most of my life. To not take my life for granted. To not waste it. To be thankful.

In much the same way, I carry with me the close calls I've had in my own life: those difficult days in ICU, the crazy traveling experiences, the countless infections where I hoped antibiotics would work for me one more time.

A few years ago, a serious urological issue caused me to slip into a seizure while at home. I awoke twelve hours later in a hospital with virtually no recollection of what happened. In the instant before the seizure happened, however, I recall thinking, *No! I'm not ready to die. How can this be? I still have so much I want to do.*

It's easy to fall into the trap of dwelling on things we cannot change or do not matter. I believe I've largely been able to overcome this by regularly reminding myself just how fortunate I am to have the life I have, and how quickly it could all be over.

Chapter Six

Hospital Tips

 ♿ Ask your doctor to prescribe a sleeping pill. There are too many noises and interruptions at night, and you need your sleep.

 ♿ Ask your doctor if you should receive a second opinion. Any good doctor will welcome a second opinion, while at the same time having confidence in his or her own opinion. It's the doctor who discourages a second opinion that you need to avoid. Merely asking the question will tell you a lot about your doctor.

 ♿ Keep a dish full of hard candy and chocolate in your room. This will encourage doctors and nurses to stop by. And it'll help treat the terminal halitosis many of them have.

 ♿ Be as involved in your medical care as possible. Learn the technical names of your injury or illness, treatments, procedures, etc.

 ♿ Learn the names of all your medications, including the dosage amount. Always check what's in the pill cup or syringe. (I've been offered the wrong pills many times.)

 ♿ Write down the names of your doctors, their specialties, and all nurses. You'll need to know these names, and will forget them if you don't write them down.

 ♿ Be skeptical of surgeons. They're trained to operate—that's what they know. And realize that many times, surgery is the wrong option.

 ♿ Ask questions of nurses. Nurses often know much more than the doctors. Avoid any doctor who disregards the opinion of a nurse or disrespects a nurse.

 ♿ Keep your dignity. They will not treat you like a piece of meat if you don't let them.

 ♿ Forget Tylenol and aspirin. If you can get real narcotics, than get them. (And intravenous drugs are better than pills.) It's unlikely you'll become addicted in a short period of time, so you might as well enjoy the ride.

 ♿ Be nice to the nurses and they'll be nice to you (e.g., visitor hours are flexible).

 ♿ Watch out for the weekends. Many doctors and nurses treat a hospital like a nine-to-five job, five days a week. Make sure you have everything you might need before 3:00 p.m. on a Friday, because you might not see anyone you recognize until Monday morning.

 ♿ Avoid having a roommate if possible. If you do have one, don't talk to them much—you'll likely regret it later. And feel free to tell them, the nurses, and the doctors if anything they do keeps you from sleeping—they might even move them.

 ♿ Put an "X2" by any item on the menu that you like. They'll usually bring you two of that item.

 ♿ Order a sandwich rather than eat shitty hospital food on the menu. (It may require the approval of a doctor or dietician.)

 ♿ There's usually a refrigerator on the floor, and you can ask to store a few goodies in it that family and friends bring you. (Again, be nice to the nurses.)

Chapter Seven

Atlanta

THE JUDER PROUDLY PUSHED her boy through the doors of Shepherd Spinal Center in Atlanta, Georgia, and it didn't take long for someone to pull her aside and scold her. "People here who can push their wheelchairs *do* push their wheelchairs," the Juder was unceremoniously informed. And with that, the tone was set. This was followed by asking me if I was registered for fall classes. "We expect you to start classes again in the fall," they instructed me.

This place is intense, I thought.

Shepherd is a lively, positive, challenging, energetic, and supportive rehabilitation hospital specializing in people with spinal cord injuries and brain injuries. They have 152 beds for inpatients, where 965 people were treated last year, as well as another 6,600 people on an outpatient basis.

Their overriding goal is to teach patients to be as independent as possible. During my time there, I learned how to dress myself, how to transfer in and out of bed and a car unassisted, how to shower alone, how to drive a van with hand controls, how to fish, to waterski, to shoot a gun, to ride an escalator, and on and on.

I met tons of people in wheelchairs who were actually *doing* things with their lives—living cool lives despite their injuries. And I heard countless stories about others doing the same.

By the time I left Shepherd, I also no longer needed to be turned every two hours when I slept; they helped me build up my skin tolerance for sleeping on one side, so I could sleep the whole night through in one position.

Yet even with all the amazing things they taught me during my two months and ten days there, it was once again something I learned outside the formal rehabilitation regimen that made the most difference. In this case, it was something I needed to learn alone.

Located in an affluent area of Atlanta called Buckhead, Shepherd provides their patients with a place to breathe some fresh air by way of a small garden which overlooks Peachtree Road. During my time at Shepherd, I probably spent as much time outside in that garden as I did in therapy. I was out there every afternoon, and I looked forward to the weekends, when I could be out there almost all day long.

I'm dating myself here, but these were the days where people listened to music on a Walkman with a long-forgotten thingamjiggy called a cassette tape. Karen had made her baby brother a mixtape with cool college music, and either it was the only tape I had or the only one I listened to. After a while, I didn't even hear the music; it simply helped to put me in some sort of trance.

What I didn't realize until I got to Shepherd was that, ever since the minute I was injured, I'd hardly had a waking minute alone. I went from the ICU to West Florida Rehab to home, all with the strong and constant support of family and friends—but I was never alone. Their support was important and needed throughout all of this, but now here I was at Shepherd all by myself. And whether I wanted to or not, it was finally time for me to really come to terms with what had happened.

I'm nineteen years old, I began a conversation with myself. *Barring some miraculous advancement in medicine, they're telling me I'll be in a wheelchair for the rest of my life. Do I really want to live like this, or should I kill myself?*

It took me years to be open with people about the fact that I contemplated killing myself. Sitting in the garden, I thought about all the ways I could do it—even with the limitations of my paralysis. Certainly there was the obvious choice of pills (I had plenty of access to those). And I could find ways to do it with a gun or knife. More nuanced, I also pondered ways I could pull it off which would make it look like an accident, so as to not hurt anyone with my suicide.

Despite these thoughts, however, I don't think I really would have categorized myself as "suicidal." In my view, I was just allowing myself the opportunity to really explore whether living like this is what I wanted to do. I was making a rational decision.

Do I want to live my life as a quadriplegic? I asked myself, just as other quadriplegics have asked. And while the cassette tape played in the background, I contemplated it fully.

It's a difficult question to seriously ask yourself: whether to live or die. But the question can't be asked by itself; it must be followed by the alternatives.

Or, if I'm not going to kill myself, I eventually continued, *how do I want to live my life?*

It took me about half of my time at Shepherd to get to the point where I was truly excited about genuinely exploring the alternatives of this second question. I then spent the second half of my time there narrowing my thoughts down to three specific questions. In many ways, these three questions have helped guide my life every day since then, and have largely brought me to where I am today:

Who do I want to be?
How do I want my family and friends to see me?
What kind of difference do I want to make with my life?

Three questions that damn near wore out my mixtape. Three questions that saved and defined a life.

MANY PEOPLE IN PENSACOLA ultimately contributed money for me to receive rehabilitation at Shepherd. All told, the bill was well over $100,000. No insurance money was involved. Mr. Chadbourne spearheaded the fundraising, although he said everyone he asked for money just pulled out their checkbook. He would have done it alone if need be, but I hope all those who contributed feel like they made a good investment. I continue to try to repay them with how I live my life.

Chapter Eight

Collegeville 3.0

TWO YEARS AND TWO MONTHS after becoming a quadriplegic, I returned to Saint Ben's/Saint John's as a student. I'd spent the better part of the first year after my accident in and out of hospitals, then began taking classes in Pensacola at the University of West Florida. (Shepherd discharged me on a Friday in time to begin classes at UWF the following Monday. No rest for the wicked!)

Like the genius I am, I returned to Minnesota from Florida in *January*. During this trip, however, there was no leaking oil or asphyxiation—the generous people of Pensacola came through yet again and made sure of that. The first Christmas I was home after my accident, people in Pensacola anonymously donated to help buy me a wheelchair accessible vehicle. Someone called my dad on Christmas Eve and told him where to look—and there, in the parking lot of his office, sat a brand new full-size van with a wheelchair lift. This was another gift that made a *huge* difference in my life.

We eventually converted the van so I could drive it. But as we drove to Collegeville, I again sat in the back the whole way. With a rear-entry wheelchair lift and the van packed to the rafters with my luggage, medical supplies, and college supplies, we would've had to unpack and repack many times for me to drive. So not only did my mom once more use her vacation days to drive her boy across the country to college, she also drove the whole way, *again*.

This time, however, Karen was with us. (And maybe she did spell the Juder once or twice with the driving, although I don't remember her doing so.) Karen is roughly two and a half years older than me in birth and seemingly two and a half feet shorter in stature. But don't let her gnome-like size fool you, she used to kick the living hell out of me growing up. Putting aside the fact that she supposedly cried for days when they brought me home from the hospital as an infant, I remember shortly after entering high school as a freshman (where Karen was a senior), Ms. Bestler, a history teacher, pulled me aside and told me frankly, "I've never seen an older sister so excited to see her brother come to high school." Yes, it's safe to say that Karen has pretty much always loved her baby brother.

Karen was a senior at Saint Mary's College in South Bend, Indiana, when I was injured. With her Thanksgiving and Christmas breaks, she was at the hospital in St. Cloud almost as much as the Juder. I used to wake up in the morning in the ICU and see her sitting beside my bed. Just knowing she was there, I could safely go back to sleep. If anything happened, she would take care of it.

As her graduation from Saint Mary's approached, all the exciting possibilities of starting a career and getting out on her own beckoned. But that's not what came first to Karen. Instead, she called my mom and told her she was coming home after graduation to help take care of me. The Juder is quick to admit that despite wanting to tell Karen she could handle it and to go on with her life, she simply said, "Okay." She was totally exhausted and needed the help.

After I returned from Shepherd, Karen and I spent pretty much every day together, all day, for over a year. The Juder would get me out of bed in the morning, and then Karen and I would eat breakfast and head to school at UWF. I initially only used a manual wheelchair because we'd not yet been given the van with a lift. So Karen not only needed to help transfer me in and out of a car countless times each day (and then load the wheelchair in and out of the car an equally large number of times) but she also had to help push my wheelchair throughout the very hilly UWF campus.

Nowadays, unless I'm traveling, I almost exclusively use an electric wheelchair. Unfortunately, some people see me in an electric wheelchair and think I'm just being lazy for not pushing my wheelchair. They watch me moving my arms and think if only I'd jump in a manual wheelchair then I'd get stronger, have huge muscular arms, and maybe win a few wheelchair races.

What they don't understand is that as a C5/C6 quadriplegic, my triceps and chest muscles were paralyzed in the same way my legs are paralyzed. It doesn't matter how many hours or how many miles I push a wheelchair, the main muscles that help push a manual wheelchair are paralyzed on me.

That being said, there are plenty of quads who use manual wheelchairs. Some do it due to the cost of an electric wheelchair, while others do it out of a sense of pride. As to the latter, they'd rather spend a chunk of their time and energy each day struggling to get from point A to point B, whereas I'd rather use that time on other things. (Besides, when you live in "East Dakota," you're dealing with snow, ice, and brutally cold temps for too many months out of the year to screw around outside trying to push icy tires with gelid hands.)

In addition to helping push my wheelchair to class, Karen also went to class with me each day, took notes for me, and—ever the better student—might have even "helped" me on a paper or exam or two.

It took me a while after my injury to learn how to write again, and longer to learn how to write quickly. But even more difficult was to learn how to study and get good grades. I wasn't much of a studier before my accident (to say the least), and it was an entirely new process for me to learn *how* to study. I certainly wasn't good at it at first. I had to keep at it.

In addition, I also had to learn how to make friends again. This took getting used to for sure. Not everyone is comfortable meeting a quadriplegic, and it took me a while to be comfortable meeting people as such. But having a bubbly, petite, chatterbox blonde always at my side served as a great icebreaker. Hell, Karen even helped me join a fraternity while at UWF. Like my father, I joined the Sigma Alpha Epsilon fraternity. Karen had to be at so many pledge events, parties, and chapter meetings, she might as well have rushed and joined SAE, too. (Phi Alpha!)

The bottom line is that without her help, there's no way I could have ever returned to Saint Ben's/Saint John's. She helped get me back into the classroom. She helped me be a better student. She helped me make friends. And most importantly, she showed me how to come through for those you love.

Never take your family for granted—whether it's before, during, or after facing one of life's challenges. The support of great friends is important to have. But there's no substitute for family. Family will come through for you when no one else will. And family will come through for you on the grandest scale.

As for Karen, I can never thank her enough for how much she helped me. I love that little talkative girl. I only wish our roles hadn't been reversed so quickly. Unfortunately, lightning can strike the same place twice.

THRILLED TO BE BACK in Collegeville, it didn't take long to become aware of the line between picking up from where I'd left off and starting over from scratch. Inherent within each year of the unique experience called "college" is the opportunity to create innumerable memories and change immeasurably. After graduation, upon being immersed into the banality of the working world, it sadly often takes decades to amass so many unforgettable moments or to experience such transformative growth. I'd been gone from CSB/SJU for over two years, and some of my pre-injury friends seemed quite different now.

Or is it me? How much have I changed? I wondered.

Certainly I looked different. Gone was the muscular, athletic boy who bounced onto campus as a freshman. Oh, I'll admit once you're in a wheelchair, it's sometimes too easy to look back on yourself and exaggerate a little. "I was an incredible athlete before my accident," I've heard too many times from my spinal cord injury brethren. *If I hadn't been injured, I'd probably be playing pro ball right now,* lingers in the minds of plenty who never had the opportunity to fail.

I was a decent athlete growing up. In high school, I played football, basketball, and ran track. If forced to pull out a glory days story, I always go with my tried-and-true tale of when I was in high school and raced NFL all-time rushing champion Emmitt Smith in the 100-yard dash. I lined up right next to him.

"Did you win?" they always ask, wide-eyed and breathlessly waiting on the edge of their seat. (I'm exaggerating.)

"No. But neither did he. He wasn't that fast." (I'm *not* exaggerating.)

I don't pretend I was a phenomenal athlete prior to my accident or that I had to beat the ladies off with a stick, but I will say I never had tons of problems meeting women. After returning to CSB/SJU from my accident, Father Cletus—the priest who promised to kick me out—never missed an opportunity to announce to a crowd that he was convinced I'd fathered half the children in St. Joseph when I was a freshman. And while he was, of course, only kidding, it highlights that I did have a few dates before I was injured. (It also highlights that the monk I saw during my first visit to Collegeville maybe wasn't so pious after all. Most brothers and priests I know at Saint John's are funny as hell. I've been fortunate enough to develop tremendous friendships with many of them. And trust me, there's no shortage in the lot that can drink, cuss, and flip you crap with the best of them.)

Returning to Saint Ben's/Saint John's as a quadriplegic, however, I found that things with the Bennies had changed quite a bit. No longer were any of them showing interest in me, and no longer did any appear receptive to my pursuits.

Molly was somewhat like my girlfriend during my freshman year. She still had a boyfriend at home but was allowed to see other people, as I had been with Nicole. Throughout the semester, we spent a lot of time together: we went to the homecoming dance together, I took her out on a few dates, and every weekend that I didn't get so drunk I ended up elsewhere, my attention was on her. (Yes, in the bizarro world that is college, this made us quite serious.)

Yet when I returned to CSB/SJU in a wheelchair, there was never so much as even a brief discussion of where we stood (not that I was standing). She was dating someone else at the time, but it was off and on. Instead, she and I just acted like old friends when around each other. And she definitely wasn't going out of her way to see her old friend.

There were also a few other past romances roaming around campus who I'd bump into from time to time. Yet it was equally clear from them: there was no spark to rekindle. They were nice. We'd talk like we had once shared a cab together, and then they'd move on.

In truth, however, that's only half the story. In fact, it's likely only ten percent of the story. For if I were to tell the full story, it would require explaining how I felt about myself, and admitting I never asked anyone out. I never really even let anyone know I might be interested. Besides, how could I ever expect a woman to be interested in me when I didn't even see myself as being worthy of their interest?

The harsh reality is that for far too long after I was injured, I more or less considered myself undesirable. Even worse, I convinced myself I was okay with that. It's not that I didn't think about women, or notice them, or wish to know them in the Biblical sense. It's just that I knew—I mean *really knew*—that they could never, ever be interested in me. I mean, how gross is that? Who the hell wants to be with a fucking quadriplegic?

SITTING IN THE GARDEN at Shepherd Spinal Center a few years earlier, the first goal I came up with was to return to Saint Ben's/Saint John's.

"I went there with the intention to graduate, and I'm not going to let this stop me," I informed Peachtree Road in Atlanta.

Before I knew it, there I was back in Collegeville, sitting in a dorm room in Benet Hall.

Each night before going to bed, I'd look in the mirror and smile. I was exhausted. I was confused. But I was starting to figure some things out. Most of all, I was very proud of myself. I'd set a goal to return to CSB/SJU and graduate. And I'd just made it through another day.

Tip #4
Establish Goals

MARK HAD BEEN A PARAPLEGIC for a little over two years, and I'd known him for less than ten minutes, when he asked me a question and then told me my answer would help him decide whether or not he was going to blow his brains out. I couldn't have then been more disgusted with myself when I realized just how quickly I allowed my own desperate search for the right answer to overshadow how desperate he must have been to ask such a horrific question of a perfect stranger.

A stout, balding white guy in his late thirties, Mark had owned a plumbing company before he was injured. Seeking to establish his credentials and former level of success, he mentioned to me repeatedly and with obvious pride that he still held the title of "Master Plumber" and that his former company had owned several trucks. I nodded my head approvingly and underscored it with a soft "Wow." I had no freakin' clue what a master plumber was, but just by the way he looked when he said it, I knew it had to be only one level below Yoda.

His tobacco-stained hands looked strong, strength undoubtedly acquired from his years as a plumber, in addition to pushing around his paralyzed body the past two years. But it was the way he fidgeted with his hands, and the way they trembled slightly that let me know that he wasn't doing well (and that was before I heard the same trembling in his voice, even before he candidly admitted it).

Certainly seeing the IV port sticking out of his wrist above his thumb may have seemed like an obvious sign of troubles, but since I had an IV port sticking out of my forearm, his port didn't seem like such a big deal. We were both patients at St. Luke's-Roosevelt Hospital in Manhattan.

Not long after his accident, his wife of seven years left him for his best friend. I tried to correct this part of his story by clarifying, "That was no best friend," but he gave me a look letting me know he'd heard that enough times by now. Besides, it's often unclear whether a relationship was wrongly defined in the past or whether it was correctly defined before and then later changed.

With his wife gone and being limited to making house calls in wheel-chair accessible homes, Mark sold his plumbing company in Long Island. He took the money and moved to Florida to start a new life.

Within a year, however, Mark had gone through all the money and ran up so much credit card debt he was forced to move back to Long Island and file for bankruptcy.

"I partied for about a year," Mark reluctantly admitted.

Having now known each other for a solid six or seven minutes, Mark began detailing for me his post-accident/post-wife sex life.

"I've been with about ten women since my accident," Mark bemoaned. "Although they were mostly one-nighters with women who just wanted to know what it's like to be with a guy in a wheelchair."

Ten women in two years?!?! I jealously thought. *Fuckin'A! That's nice work, Holmes.*

"But I'm tired of all these one-night stands," a suddenly pensive Mark/Ron Jeremy reflected. "I'm looking for something that's more long-term. Besides, I've tried all the different types of Viagra pills and shots, but my erections don't last long. Don't get me wrong, I love eating [insert the alternate name for kittens], but me and my wife used to fuck like an-imals. I miss fucking."

Without skipping a beat, Mark then changed course. He exercised his right as a card-carrying member of the Wheelchair Club:

"Why are you in a chair?" he asked.

Not unlike the freedom black people enjoy in using the "N-word" whenever they want, when you're in a wheelchair, you don't need to be careful about asking someone else why they're in a chair. You're a member of the club.

My response that my neck had been broken in a Full Nelson wrestling hold typically catches people by surprise. Mark was somewhat impressed, but not unduly so. On the contrary, it was obvious he was ashamed of how he was injured.

"I've done some bad things," he began. "I was buying cocaine in a house one night after work. There was a drive-by shooting, and a bullet came through the wall and hit me. I'd never been to that house before in my life."

Shifting gears yet again, he wanted to know all I'd done with my life since my accident. I obliged him with a quick overview and his eyes began to water. It was then that he posed the question to me:

"You've been in a wheelchair for a long time, Bob. What do you think is going to happen to me? Because I'll tell you what, if I can't figure it out by the time I'm discharged from the hospital in a few days, the first thing I plan to do is take a gun and blow my brains out."

I had to consider my answer carefully, to say the least. But the perfect way to respond to him was actually quite obvious. I'd been trained by the best to know exactly how to handle this:

"Mark, I have to be honest with you," I began gently. "I think you're the asshole of the whole world."

Wait. No. That was the line from my psychologist at West Florida Rehab. Only a true professional can deliver a line like that.

Instead, I began thinking long and hard for an answer. I was instantly awash in my own sea of self-doubt—completely overwhelmed by the enormity, gravity, and finality of my answer. The level of desperation Mark most certainly had reached to ask his question was now lost. I'd completely forgotten about him. It was now all about me. Would my answer be brilliant or idiotic? Legendary or notorious? Heroic or catastrophic?

Holy shit, Mark! This is a lot of goddamn pressure on me, I whined to myself. *How the hell am I supposed to know what's going to happen to you? I just met your sorry ass ten minutes ago.*

But then it came to me. My answer popped into my head and instantly I landed on rock-solid ground. I was sure this was how I should answer him.

"You need to get a job, Mark," I said with the utmost of confidence. "I don't care if it's as a telemarketer or a greeter at Walmart. You need a reason to get out of bed each morning. Maybe you can work in the plumbing department at Home Depot? I don't know. But what I do know is that you need some sort of purpose to your life. When you get out of here, Mark, you need to find a job."

WORKING TOWARD A GOAL is one of the best ways I know to avoid getting bogged down in self-pity while facing one of life's challenges. You need to have something to look forward to, something to be excited about. You need a reason to want to get out of bed in the morning. Working toward whatever this *something* is provides purpose to your effort each day.

It's easier to prepare yourself for the daily fight knowing your effort is moving you one step closer to, or actually experiencing, whatever it is that brings you happiness, excitement, pride, joy, laughter.

I felt confident about my advice to Mark because having a job is often so elemental to having a sense of purpose, and it goes a long way in defining who you are.

For the majority of hours most people are awake, they're at their job. How can this be anything other than a large part of one's identity when it makes up such a large part of each day?

Sometimes in life, when the inspiration to keep going is at its lowest, simply needing to show up at work is enough of a push. At least it's a starting point—a point from which to build. And in Mark's case, there was also the practical aspect: he needed money to pay the bills.

But a job certainly doesn't require monetary compensation to provide a sense of purpose. Volunteering is a job. Being a stay-at-home parent is a job (often one of the hardest jobs). Anything where someone, anyone, is relying on you, counting on you to show up, or will ultimately benefit from your effort, is all that you need to provide you with a sense of purpose.

And despite the fact that many people are reluctant to accept it, whatever job you choose to do defines who you are to a considerable extent. If you say you're a brain surgeon, people have a preconceived notion of who you are. If you say you're a mailman, people will judge you based on this information alone. The simple labeling of people based on their occupation is unavoidable and undeniable.

The beauty of accepting all this for what it is, is that you're then empowered to decide what you want your purpose to be, and how you wish to be defined.

For life's truly fortune-favored, these worlds exist in the same sphere. These people find true purpose in what they do, and they're comfortable with how others define them.

In today's society, however, achieving this goal is often unrealistic. In order to afford everything they want for themselves or for their family, people choose a job that in itself doesn't provide them much by way of a sense of purpose. Their job is *just* a job—a means to an end.

But a job failing to *provide* a sense of purpose by no means indicates that it *serves* no purpose. Quite to the contrary, such a job often aids people in pursuing their true purpose—e.g., supporting their family, having access to good health insurance, helping to save money, providing greater quality of life.

So regardless of whether your job helps you pursue your purpose directly or indirectly, simply through the act of going to work each day, you're making advancements toward achieving your goal. These daily successes (or these daily opportunities to inch closer toward success) help counterbalance the effort required to face the challenges of each day.

And yet, a job is but only one example of a goal to work toward. It could be that your goal is to go back to school. Maybe learning a new language is something you want to accomplish. Taking a vacation in an exotic locale is one of my personal favorites—a goal definitely worthy of pursuit, and something to look forward to emphatically!

At certain points in life, however, your goal may end up being as basic as simply wanting to make it through the day. And when that day is over, you will have a wonderful feeling of accomplishment. You did it! Some of my initial days returning to Collegeville were spent achieving these very types of goals.

It has been my experience, though, that working toward longer-term goals—those that require steadfast, tedious, meticulous, and arduous attention over a prolonged period of time—often prove to be the most rewarding. The most worthwhile accomplishments usually require the hardest work. That's why so few are able to achieve them.

Working toward longer-term goals also allows you to put into perspective whatever challenge you're facing. Time shows no preference in its relentlessness—it simply persists and endures no matter what. Embracing this truth empowers you to pursue whatever goal you desire with the confidence you can pursue it as relentlessly as time itself. And as the years clip by, you'll hopefully be able to look back on goals you met which at first seemed daunting or insurmountable, yet wore down with time and became manageable.

This of course holds equally true for facing life's challenges: they may seem daunting and insurmountable at first, but time will wear them down, too—and they will become manageable.

So get started today. Use that ticking clock to your advantage. Spend time pursuing things that make you want to get out of bed in the morning. I promise you'll quickly find yourself focusing on the positive rather than the negative.

Chapter Nine

St. Joseph

WHEREAS SAINT JOHN'S IS ENSCONCED within 2,700 acres of pine trees, wetlands, prairies, and lakes, Saint Ben's is slap dab in the middle of the thriving metropolis of St. Joseph, Minnesota—a city offering everything any college student could ever possibly want.

At Bo Diddley's you can scarf an amazing mayonnaise-slathered sub sandwich dripping with some sort of Italian salad dressing. At Gary's Pizza you can achieve the full freshman fifteen by mowing down on the best 'za that side of College Avenue. At the El Paso you can bowl or play beach volleyball with your friends when you should be studying. And at Kay's Kitchen you can step back in time (circa 1972) to savor an afternoon char-broiled burger, or meet there in the morning, hungover, in much need of a killer greasy breakfast.

For the avant-garde, you can grab a cup of joe at the Local Blend while checking out some artisanal wares and listening to live music. Or you can impress a date by sharing a romantic dinner at Bella Cucina—possibly even eating outside if it's above freezing. (I highly recommend the calamari.)

But it's the most time-honored tradition of where you choose to imbibe that announces to the world who you are. Sal's, the La Playette, the Legion, or the Midway? It's an important choice—for it largely encapsulates where you stand politically, if not socioeconomically and spiritually. Or . . . it might just be where the drink special is that night.

(Ah, the college life!)

My senior year of college I was asked to sit on a panel discussing diversity at Saint Ben's/Saint John's. The event was being held at Saint Ben's on a mid-April night, about a month before my graduation.

Everyone speculated that it would turn into a conversation about race—and ultimately a black/white thing. Many of the black students weren't pleased with being the overwhelming minority at a very white school, in a very white city, in a very white state. Those statistics have fortunately all softened a good bit since that time, but they were stark back then.

Eventually, a black student named Larry from Chicago stepped to the microphone to voice his frustration. He'd recently been pulled over while driving in St. Cloud for no apparent reason other than being black. He also felt students and professors treated him differently based on his color, and he was tired of all this.

Larry was a junior and said that in twenty-seven days, when the semester was over, he was transferring out of CSB/SJU and heading back to Chicago.

"Twenty-seven days," Larry repeated over and over. "And I can go back to a place where people will not act differently around me just because I'm black. Twenty-seven days and I can leave a place that never accepted me because I'm black. Twenty-seven days."

I sat there at the panelist table listening to all this. *How different is his situation from mine?* I thought. *Do I have the right to even draw an analogy on this? After all, I'm not black, and I have no idea what it feels like to be black.*

Ultimately, I couldn't restrain myself. I had to speak. I leaned into the microphone and gave a blanket disclaimer:

"I'm not black, and I have no idea what it feels like to be black," I began. "But I know what it feels like to be discriminated against. I know what it feels like to have someone look at you and then judge you without knowing anything about you. I know what it's like to have people feel uncomfortable around you when you've done nothing but enter the room. I know what it's like to have people stare at you, to talk about you behind your back when you pass by. I've heard many a child say, 'Look at him, Mommy. What's wrong with him?' And I've shown up at countless restaurants and businesses and been turned away. They didn't say, 'We don't serve your kind.' Instead they said, 'I'm sorry, we're not wheelchair accessible.'

"But I also know that since coming back to CSB/SJU, they've put an electric door on Benet Hall at SJU. And I'm not claiming to be Rosa Parks, but there's now also a lift on one of the buses—so I'm able to ride between campuses like everyone else.

"But most importantly, if one person—only one person—has gotten to know me, and based on knowing me is now more comfortable around people in wheelchairs, then I feel like I've made a difference. I feel like I made a difference to that individual, as well as for the next person in a wheelchair they meet. And I hope I've done my part to make it easier for the next person who goes to CSB/SJU in a wheelchair.

"Twenty-seven days and I will have accomplished something that was so much harder than I ever thought it would be when I began here. Twenty-seven days and I will be able to look at myself in the mirror and know I didn't quit.

"Twenty-seven days."

And with that I passed back the microphone.

I don't know if I was really talking to Larry or finally realizing something for myself. My aim was to point out just how precious a gift it is to be afforded an opportunity to *actually* make a difference. I could have stayed at the University of West Florida where my tuition was paid for by vocational rehabilitation of Florida, where the weather was much nicer, and where there were many people in wheelchairs on campus. It would have been easier.

But instead I chose to finish what I started at CSB/SJU. While I was student there, I was the only person in a wheelchair at the whole school. According to some older priests, only three students in wheelchairs had preceded me. By the time I left, however, a few changes on campus had been made that I know were brought about because of my advocacy, or because others recognized my needs on their own, and then made the effort to address the issues.

Similarly, never a day goes by where I enter a public establishment or use an accessible bathroom that I don't quietly thank those in wheelchairs who preceded me—for they made my life so much easier.

I was injured in November of 1989. Less than one year later, in July of 1990, George H.W. Bush signed into law the Americans with

Disabilities Act (ADA). The first few years after I was injured, I can't tell you the number of times I went to a restaurant and the waiter or waitress would take the order of whomever I was with, then look at me, and then look back to the other person and say, "And what will *he* have?"

"Well, *he* can speak. Why don't you ask *him*?" either my companion or I would lightheartedly apprise the server.

Nowadays, that never happens to me. People see me as a paying customer. I believe the ADA exemplifies the best of what citizen advocacy and Washington can accomplish. It's often too easy to be cynical about our politicians, even with conceding that such cynicism has been largely well placed. But laws can and do change lives.

Similarly, the contributions of Hollywood, the media, and responsible businesses should not be overlooked. Casting the role of someone in a wheelchair humanizes the predicament and subconsciously makes it seem more ordinary. Likewise, it's hard to find a commercial from Nike, McDonald's, Walmart, and many others, where someone in a wheelchair isn't in the background or the focus of the ad. These things matter. Over the last twenty-plus years, from the vantage point of my own wheelchair, I've witnessed firsthand how people's perception of me has changed.

There are so many people to thank for this. And I've tried my best to make them proud by embracing the opportunities their efforts have afforded me. At the same time, I've endeavored to make my own contributions. As is so often the case, I'm the only one in a wheelchair in a class, at a party, at an event, at my job, traveling, and elsewhere. I've strived to never shy away from the challenges presented to me in each new environment. And while I'm often the first person in a wheelchair many people have met, I've tried to be a good ambassador when forging new ground. I've simply tried my damndest to make it easier for those who follow me.

With all that having been said, I'm afraid I have a confession to make: I didn't actually say any of what's written above to Larry. Like so many times in life, I thought of it too late. As I drove back to Collegeville from St. Joe, it dawned on me what I should have said to Larry.

At the time, I considered writing an article in the school newspaper to try to make my views heard. But finals soon became the priority, and it slipped away. In writing this chapter, however, I received another precious gift, and one of life's rarities: a second bite at the apple.

Missed opportunities are rarely seen again. (Sorry, Larry.)

TWENTY-SEVEN DAYS LATER, I graduated from Saint John's University, one year later than I would have if I hadn't been injured. I never received below a 3.5 GPA during any semester upon my return. I majored in accounting and landed a job with a prestigious accounting firm before Thanksgiving of my senior year. The Juder, Karen, my dad, and my stepmom were all there to see me graduate. It remains one of the proudest moments of my whole life.

At graduation from SJU with the Juder, my stepmom, my dad, and Karen.

Chapter Ten

Minneapolis

K AREN WAS DIAGNOSED with cancer the summer between my junior and senior years at Saint Ben's/Saint John's. After helping me return to Collegeville, she resumed her life by moving to Washington, D.C., and working for an attorney who specialized in disabilities law.

Stress no doubt exacerbated the spread of her cancer, while some argue it actually caused the cancer. Her boss was quite demanding, and the guy she was dating—an unemployed, uneducated, unmotivated, unattractive, unfunny, unacceptable ex-bartender—was, by all accounts and without any exceptions, an absolute loser. And that's being kind.

She didn't think it strange that she woke up in the middle of each night to change her bedding, having sweated through her sheets once again. It was summertime in D.C., after all, and she had no air conditioning.

Feeling exhausted all the time certainly frustrated her. But she was working hard at her job, and desperately trying to deworm her dog of a boyfriend.

Her growing propensity for bruising did not go unnoticed. But then again, our granny, the Juder's mother, always bruised easily. Maybe at the ripe old age of twenty-three, Karen's skin was thinning, too. Certainly the dentist she visited for a cleaning in Washington didn't help her with this clue. She returned to his office the next day with a black-and-blue face. His only concern was with not being blamed for a rough check-up.

It was when she found a lump on her breast that she finally went to see a doctor. It wasn't a tumor, though. It was a mass of white blood cells. She was diagnosed with leukemia—cancer of the blood and bone marrow.

I remember like it was yesterday, sitting on the phone, listening to Karen and her new oncologist at George Washington University Hospital in Washington, D.C. Dr. Broome was patiently explaining the impending process: regimens of chemotherapy, months in and out of the hospital, extreme nausea, and susceptibility to infections (it being too soon for technical explanations of neutropenic sepsis—infections that occur in patients with no immune system).

Karen's voice was strong throughout the call. After all, this wasn't our family's first rodeo. But when she mentioned one of the side effects of her treatment, she finally broke down.

"I'm going to lose all my hair," wept my sister with long, blonde hair.

When we hung up the phone, I watched as the Juder's head slunk forward. With Karen no longer on the phone, she lost the strength to even hold up her head.

I was living at home in Pensacola for the summer. The Juder was taking care of me morning and night as she continued to work at the bank. I was on the phone in my bedroom that our architect, Brian, helped us build, and the Juder was in the kitchen on a separate phone. Over three years had passed since her son had become a quadriplegic. I could see her through the kitchen window as she began to bear this new weight thrust upon her; it was obvious she wasn't ready to carry any more.

I rolled from my bedroom into the kitchen and sat beside her.

"I cain't lose'er. I *just cain't* lose her," was all she could muster through a broken heart.

WHEN ASKED DURING the interview if I could fly, I knew a job offer from Arthur Andersen was forthcoming. Their concern was that someone in a wheelchair wouldn't be able to fly on an airplane from Minneapolis to Chicago in order to attend their training center in St. Charles, Illinois.

"No, I can't fly," I answered, smiling coyly and with my voice dripping with sarcasm. "Can *you* fly?"

Channeling Peter Pan during a job interview isn't always a good idea. But in this case it worked—a job offer to work at Arthur Andersen soon followed. Of course I let them know that I'd flown on airplanes several times since being in a wheelchair. But their question served to broadly underscore the unfamiliar ground on which they were embarking by hiring someone on wheels.

I called the Juder and Karen at the hospital to let them know the good news. With bags of antibiotics, blood transfusions, and chemotherapy festooning the IV pole beside Karen's bed, any drop of good news was eagerly welcomed.

In the coming weeks, my decision of which job offer to accept became obvious. During the interview process, I mentioned to each potential employer that Minnesota was spending a large amount of money on me for my medical care, supplies, and what not, and I wasn't sure if that would continue when I started receiving a salary.

Despite being well aware I was still interviewing with the other prestigious accounting firms, the people at Arthur Andersen hired a consultant to help me with this process. They then called me and said I could meet with this consultant whenever I wanted, and that all expenses were paid regardless of whether or not I accepted their offer.

"Where you choose to work is up to you," they told me. "We just want to make sure you understand everything as best as possible."

And with that, my decision was made. I chose Arthur Andersen. As I began working there, however, a very interesting phenomenon became totally apparent to me. Once noticed, I realized it's a phenomenon that has remained consistent in every new environment I've entered as someone in wheelchair, even going back to my return to Saint Ben's/Saint John's.

The phenomenon is this: *Being in a wheelchair is one of the greatest litmus tests in the world to reveal confident people and expose insecure people.*

Over my lifetime in a wheelchair, I've found that confident people—people secure in who they are—are without question the first people to gravitate towards me (and give me a fair shot) when I enter a new environment. Fortunately, and I guess rather expectedly, these are also the people who everyone likes and wants to be around. They're charismatic, confident, and comfortable in their own skin. These people see me and recognize (consciously or subconsciously) that others are uncomfortable around me, and that many are intentionally avoiding me. I'm someone outside the comfort zone of most people—that is, unless they've had previous exposure.

This scenario has played itself out so many times for me that it's now quite predictable: these confident people give me enough of a chance for them to recognize I'm the coolest dude on the face of the planet (or, if that's a wee bit of an exaggeration, at least I'm better than the insecure wannabes kissing their ass). The confident people then start spending time with me, and then guess what? You guessed it— the insecure people then also want to be friends with the new guy in the wheelchair.

"I have a friend in a wheelchair," these lame posers casually drop to anyone who'll listen. "But I don't even see the wheelchair."

It's comical and I love it.

That said, it is true of those who have sincerely taken the time to get to know me well—they actually don't see the wheelchair anymore. These close friends and family tell me continuously (through their actions and words) that they see me for who I am, not the chair I sit in.

The entire process is revealing and highly entertaining—a truly spectacular side benefit to being in a wheelchair.

As for dear ole Arthur Andersen, I worked in their corporate tax department for almost four years and then left to attend law school. I was doing a lot of legal research and writing of memos while there, and I figured I might as well go to law school and learn what the hell this was really all about. I also didn't really enjoy doing taxes so much. The Juder thought it was a huge mistake for me to leave Arthur Andersen. A few years after I left, however, they went out of business. The Enron scandal and a host of other problems brought it down. It's disappointing, though. It was a great company. (It also shows that moms aren't right about everything.)

During my time working at Arthur Andersen, I went to their training center in St. Charles, Illinois, twice. I drove there from Minneapolis in my van both times.

KAREN REQUIRED THREE SEPARATE sessions of chemotherapy over about a nine-month period of time. The first two sessions went relatively well. She was in for a month or so, then out for a month or so, then back in. I was with her in the hospital as much as possible (desperately trying to return the favor for all she did for me), but I wasn't there nearly enough.

As a family, we contemplated whether I'd return to Saint Ben's/Saint John's for my senior year or stay in Washington to help Karen. Returning to Collegeville seemed like the best decision, especially because if I stayed in D.C., my mom would need to take care of me *and* help Karen. The Juder was on another fully paid leave of absence from her generous bank in Pensacola. There was of course no debating whether she was going to be with Karen at the hospital the whole time like she had been for me. The Juder wouldn't have it any other way.

It was during Karen's third session of chemotherapy that things took a terrible turn. Having already endured two beatings from chemotherapy, her body basically lacked any immune system (neutropenia), and she developed a fungal infection in her lungs (aspergillus). Compounding this quagmire was also the fact that her blood lacked virtually all clotting ability (thrombocytopenia, or reduced platelet count).

Day after day she ran a terrible fever and these infections were taking a toll. The doctors threw every antibiotic combination/concoction they could think of at her, but nothing seemed to help.

Eventually it came down to a choice: perform a surgery at 6:00 a.m. the next morning where they would go in and remove a piece of her lung for a biopsy, or continue trying to treat her blindly with antibiotics. The problem with the surgery, however, was that Karen lacked enough platelets to clot her blood, so she'd likely bleed to death on the operating table. And the problem with continuing to treat her with antibiotics was that they weren't working. Either way, the surgery or the infection was likely going to kill her within the next twenty-four hours.

That was the news I received during a phone call with Karen and my mom during my last semester at Saint Ben's/Saint John's. Karen would likely die in the next twenty-four hours.

Listening to Karen on the phone, I could hear the fear in her voice. She told me in a quivering tone of a doctor who had come to see her that day and candidly informed her, "You're deteriorating right in front of our eyes."

Unfortunately, I could hear that same deterioration in her will to keep fighting. There seemed an obvious amount of quit in her voice. Without a doubt, she was exhausted. She was scared. Her body was ravaged by cancer, infection, and countless medications. Anyone in her position would experience the same thing. But in my heart, I still wanted to challenge her to keep up the fight. *Don't give up! Stay strong!* I desperately wanted to urge her. I wanted to try to push her in the most loving way possible—to encourage her when she so clearly needed encouraging.

But instead, as we ended our conversation, contemplating that this may be the last time I ever spoke to my sister, I took the easy way out: I told her how much I loved her. I didn't challenge her at all. The last thing I wanted was a final memory of speaking to my sister and giving her a hard time. It didn't seem right.

And with that, we hung up.

That's when the Juder took over.

The decision of whether or not to have surgery was left entirely in my mom's hands. Karen was certainly old enough to make the decision, but her mother was still very much just that: her mother.

The Juder went outside to smoke a cigarette, and when she returned, she was full of nothing but piss and vinegar.

"Ya know what'chur problem is?" she began with her smoke-break lecture prepared. "Ya lie dare in dat bed an' look like ya dyin'. The doctors come'n here an' see ya lookin' like dat, an' dats all day can thank 'bout. Well, lemme tell ya what. Fo' now on, when people come in da room, ya gonna smile, ya gonna be cheery, ya gonna ask dem how day doin', an' ya gonna look cute. Ya need ta let 'em know dat ya very much alive an' ya wanna live! An' sumptin' else: ya not gonna always be in dat bed, neither. No wonder ya sick—ya never get any exercise. Ya need ta start gettin' outta dat bed more. An' ya need start thinkin' 'bout gettin' outta here. Ya had dose financial aid forms fo' months. So tonight, we gonna start

78

fillin' dem out. An' every thirty minutes, ya gonna get outta dat bed. I don't care if it's to walk 'round da utta side. But'cha will get out dat bed!"

At the time, Karen was contemplating going back to graduate school. She'd even gone so far as receiving the financial aid forms from Emory University in Atlanta, Georgia, where she was considering a master's in hospital administration.

With her smoke-break lecture having now been delivered, the Juder proudly left the room, heading back outside for another smoke break.

A few minutes later, a nurse entered the room and noticed Karen looked a bit different.

"What's going on with you?" the nurse inquired.

"My mom just kicked my ass," a smiling Karen chuckled.

The Juder and Karen stayed up well past midnight that night filling out financial aid forms. The Juder had made the call: there would be no 6:00 a.m. surgery. It was too soon to decide whether the antibiotics were working. Her daughter needed to fight harder first.

The next day, Karen's health improved. In fact, it improved every day after that. About a month later, she was discharged from the hospital—cancer free!

A FEW DAYS BEFORE FINALS during the fall semester of my third year of law school at the University of Minnesota, I received a phone call from the U.S. Securities and Exchange Commission in Washington, D.C. They'd received my application and asked to interview me in Washington. They were flexible about when I scheduled my interview, but admitted to filling positions on a rolling basis—meaning as soon as the positions were filled, my offer to interview would expire.

Of course I wanted to wait until finals were over to interview. I also didn't have anyone to help with my medical care who could go with me on such short notice. Besides, I didn't have enough money to purchase a plane ticket for immediate use—let alone money for two of these tickets.

What I did have, however, were enough frequent flyer miles for one ticket, which could be purchased immediately. I fortunately also had enough life experiences behind me to know that sometimes, you just need to suck it up, and taking a calculated risk or two can pay off.

So, within a day or two of receiving the offer to interview, I woke up early on a late December Minnesota morning, had my caregiver help me put on a suit, drove to the airport in my electric wheelchair, parked my van, boarded a plane to Washington, arrived in D.C. that afternoon with my wheelchair intact, took the Metro to GW Hospital (a place I knew well from all of Karen's treatment there), found an empty waiting room in the hospital, and sat there in my wheelchair all night. I never slept a wink.

Around 7:00 a.m., I filed off the stubble on my face with an electric razor, dropped some Visine in my red eyes, took a caffeine pill, and asked a nurse to button my top button and straighten my tie.

I interviewed with the SEC that morning and was back in Minneapolis later that evening—greeted at the airport in Minnesota with temperatures dangerously below zero and a wheelchair severely damaged in the flight. (If the damage had happened in reverse order, the entire trip would have been ruined.)

I received a job offer from the SEC the day after my interview. My next stage in life was to become a securities lawyer in Washington.

Five months later, I graduated *cum laude* from the University of Minnesota Law School. I may be in the minority with this feeling, but I enjoyed law school immensely. It taught me a tremendous amount about reading critically, structuring arguments logically, articulating my thoughts coherently, and (hopefully) writing clearly.

The Juder, Karen, my dad, and my stepmom were once again at my graduation. For my graduation present, I asked the Juder to buy me a class ring—not from the University of Minnesota, but from Saint John's. They had recently created a very distinctive class ring, one prominently featuring the bell banner and honeycomb wall.

At my graduation party, with a variety of family and friends gathered, I told them I planned to move to Washington, then to New York, and then to come back to teach at Saint Ben's/Saint John's—all within the next ten years. I'd set another goal for myself. It was long-term, and it was audacious.

I called it "The Ten-Year Plan."

Chapter Eleven

Beaver Dam

Beaver Dam, Wisconsin, population 16,234, is home to one of the finest wheelchair ramps ever built. It makes me feel better to think it still stands, although I'm sure it was taken down not long after it was built. It was constructed hastily by someone with no prior experience in ramp building, but who accepted the job because of an open mind. Today the wood it was made of is likely quite splintered and weathered, and it was never built to pass any ADA code. But it's a ramp that completely changed the way I saw myself then, as well as how I see myself today—at least whenever I think of that ramp.

The summer between my second and third years in law school, I worked on Capitol Hill in Washington, D.C., for Senator Bob Graham from Florida. My tax experience at Arthur Andersen combined with my law student credentials and some strong references from Pensacola helped me land this opportunity. (Of course, my willingness to work for virtually no pay likely cemented the deal.) My summer internship was spent working on issues running through the Senate Finance Committee.

Ann was my caregiver for the summer. She was twenty-one years old, dishwater blonde, full of laughter, laid back yet always up for a party, and very cute. She had a broad smile, freckled cheeks, and a small athletic frame with rounded shoulders, drawn forward due to fortunate, well-placed weight.

The funny thing is, I didn't really know her until she sat down in the passenger seat of my van and we began driving from Minneapolis to Washington for the summer. Her sister went to the University of Minnesota and was one of my caregivers. Ann was about to enter her senior year at Marquette University in Milwaukee, Wisconsin, where she was majoring in dental hygiene. (Yes, it appears that's a four-year major). Ann's sister more or less convinced her to take the job.

It was during our two-day drive to Washington that my Ten-Year Plan dawned on me and began to hatch. I knew I loved Saint Ben's/Saint John's—my experience there transformed me as a person. Certainly my injury played a part in this, but it largely only helped to open my eyes to what should have been obvious anyway.

Instead, my growth was primarily fueled by forming soul-piercing, lifelong friendships; by witnessing the profound dedication, faith, and joy of the monastics; by being supported and challenged by the professors; and by feeling humbled, inspired, and blessed to know so many amazing people working for and associated with these two schools.

Suddenly, my search for a way to make a difference with my life was abundantly clear. Contributing back to a place that had given so much to me would be both an honor and a privilege. I knew firsthand the extraordinary difference CSB/SJU made in the lives of so many. I was awestruck to think I might have the opportunity to play a part in doing the same.

Fortunately, I also felt confident that with my law degree and enough work experience, I'd be given a fair shot at CSB/SJU in the Accounting and Finance Department. And so this caregiver, whom I'd essentially just met, was forced to hear me ramble on for a two-day drive to Washington about The Ten-Year Plan.

IF THIS BOOK WERE NOT dedicated to the Juder, it would definitely be dedicated to my caregivers. Over the past twenty-plus years of being in a wheelchair, I've had over one hundred caregivers. Their ages, races, ethnicities, genders, sexual orientations, educations, and lots in life have spanned the full panoply of all that makes life interesting.

Yet one common thread weaves them all together: these people understand that small acts can *and do* make a big difference.

During my summer at Shepherd Spinal Center, they taught me countless ways I could be fully independent—to live each day without the assistance of caregivers. At my level of injury, it is *possible* for me to transfer myself in and out of bed, dress and undress, bathe, and take care of my bodily functions, all without the assistance of anyone. (Just knowing this is a possibility is more liberating than you can imagine.)

While at Shepherd, I relished every bit of knowledge they provided me, and took advantage of trying everything I could. I tried tons of things that failed. But I learned many things that worked only after they had failed several times earlier. When all was said and done, it was up to me to decide which of these successes to implement into my daily routine. In several areas of my life, I've chosen to use caregivers rather than spend the time and energy trying to do certain things myself. Granted, it may not be much of a choice in that if I attempted to do these things myself, the quality of care would decline precipitously just as the risk of injury would rise dramatically, not to mention the significant investment of time. But the feeling as though I have a *choice* in this matter is something that means the world to me. (Never take for granted the luxury of a choice.)

If a caregiver helps me to bed at night, it can take as little as half an hour from the time they arrive until lights out. If a caregiver helps me out of bed in the morning, I can be out of bed and in my wheelchair in two hours or less, depending on the day. Of course two hours in the morning just to get out of bed may seem like a lot of time, but if I were to try to do it myself, it could easily take four or five hours, and the quality of care would suffer greatly. Similarly, going to bed at night without a caregiver would likely stretch closer to two hours, and my level of comfort, safety, and care would be poor at best. Finally, throw fashion into this equation, and the decision for me is quite clear: if I were to dress and undress myself, wearing velcro shoes and sweatpants would be the most expedient. And this player has way too much style for that bull-malarkey. Most days I wear a full suit with a tie. (Pimpin' ain't easy!)

Therefore, since the day I left Shepherd, whether it be the Juder or one of the over one hundred other amazing individuals I've had the pleasure to know, I've *chosen* to rely on caregivers for much of my personal care. It is a choice that has been both a blessing and a curse.

The overriding curse is that it has put me in the position to experience some of the most vulnerable, embarrassing, humiliating, demeaning and degrading situations I wouldn't wish on my worst enemy. Yet it has been a blessing in allowing me to live a more "normal" life despite my injury—affording me enough hours in the day to do well in school, have a demanding full-time job, be active with my friends, travel, and live a fuller life.

Additionally, in a bizarre way, with as bad as the daily reliance on other people for personal care can be, it has served to inspire me to try to make the most out of each day.

If you're gonna endure this, I often say to myself, *you better feel good about what you're doing with the rest of your day.* I feel this daily reminder has helped to keep me focused on really enjoying my life, making it count, and being proud of my decisions.

At the same time, many of my caregivers have been extraordinary people who I would likely never have had the chance to get to know. I've developed lots of great friendships over the years with many of them. The nights or mornings they've helped me were times I looked forward to. We laugh, share frustrations, solve problems, and then laugh some more. Receiving their help often feels more like a social hour than a medical necessity. To them, I owe a special debt of gratitude.

But every one of my caregivers faced the predicament so often thrust upon each of us. In his famous "I've Been to the Mountaintop" speech, delivered the day before his assassination in 1968, Martin Luther King, Jr., paraphrased the Biblical tale of the Good Samaritan, which describes this predicament:

> The first question which the priest and the Levite asked was: "If I stop to help this man, what will happen to me?" But . . . the good Samaritan reversed the question and asked: "If I do not stop to help this man, what will happen to him?"

My life has been elevated beyond my dreams because each of my caregivers asked what would happen to me if they did not help. Most of them have been college students, making a few bucks, gaining some experience, or volunteering. Each of them helped me for only a short period of time (most for a few semesters; some for a few years). They all move on after a while. Yet if you were to look closely at my entire life in a wheelchair, you would find within it a traceable, significant, and irreplaceable contribution made by each of them. The small acts by these phenomenal individuals absolutely, positively *has* made a big difference! Because when you combine each of their acts together, you'll find that it changed the life of a very appreciative guy in a wheelchair for twenty-four years and counting.

During that time, I've been fortunate enough to lead an amazing life, achieve extraordinary goals, and experience so much happiness. It is largely on the broad shoulders of my caregivers that I've been lifted to such incredible heights.

MY SUMMER WITH ANN in Washington moved beyond her simply being my caregiver. Within a few weeks, a night of heavy drinking ended with the two of us waking up together in bed, tender from a case of carpet tunnel syndrome. In my previous ten years in a wheelchair, I hadn't gone out on a single date with a woman, much less had a girlfriend or found myself waking up in bed with someone. But here we were, living together for the next several months in an apartment at Georgetown's Law School.

I remember going to a grocery store together later that afternoon to buy our food for the week. *Holy shit! I'm living with my girlfriend!* I marveled to myself.

Needless to say, the summer of 2000 was awesome. Ann had the most amazing capacity of seeing the best in people. Regardless of the person or the situation, she saw beauty in people in a way I had no idea existed. And despite never wanting a caregiver to also be my significant other, she was able to care for me in a manner that made my spinal cord injury seem like no big deal. She viewed caring for me simply as an extension of me, and it was clear it was never a burden or hassle for her. There were certain times she looked at me, or in the way she acted around me, that literally took my breath away.

Being with Ann taught me for the first time that I could actually be a good partner to someone, regardless of my wheelchair, which was something I'd given up hope on years ago (if such hope ever even existed). Certainly becoming more comfortable exploring my physical abilities was enormously important. But Ann and I were simply having a blast together as a couple. And with the two of us being only eight years apart in age, after a while I couldn't help but wonder if she was "the one."

Yet as the summer wound down on Capitol Hill, despite caring for Ann a great deal, my gut told me we weren't meant for each other—or at least, not right then. She still had her senior year of college ahead of her, and I knew my third year of law school would be busy. As we planned for our drive back to Minneapolis, my mind was pretty well made up as to where we stood. I planned to break up with her shortly after we resumed our lives at school. (Not that, of course, I discussed any of that with her.)

A few days before leaving Washington, Ann asked if it would be okay if we spent one night at her parents' house on our way back. Beaver Dam, Wisconsin, wasn't exactly on the way, but it wasn't far out of the way, either. It extended a two-day trip into three days, but that wasn't a big deal.

Driving up to front of the house days later, the first thing I saw was many stairs leading to the front door. I'd forgotten to ask if her parents' house was even wheelchair accessible, and it appeared it was not.

Maybe we'll just meet her parents at a restaurant and then keep going, I thought, if not somewhat hoped. But Ann said she thought we would likely be able to enter in the back.

Rolling over the freshly cut grass in my wheelchair, I rounded the corner to the backyard of her house and my stomach sank to my ankles. Attached to the back of the house was a brand new ramp. It was made of wood that had clearly never seen a drop of rain nor withstood a harsh ray of sunshine.

Feeling so guilty I could hardly swallow, I pathetically asked, "Do you have a relative in a wheelchair?"

But the ramp had been built for me.

I knew full well Ann and her mother communicated regularly throughout the summer. In fact, her mother had even visited us in

Washington. So when it came time for Ann's new boyfriend to visit the family home in Beaver Dam, discussions about accessibility likely then ensued.

I had yet to meet Ann's father, though. But despite whatever concerns or misgivings he may have had over his daughter dating a quadriplegic, he built a ramp for my entrance. To be totally fair to him, however, as well as to the rest of the family, after spending the night at their home in Beaver Dam, it was clear none of them had any concerns or misgivings at all—even as inconceivable as that seemed to me. The whole family welcomed me into their home with a completely open mind.

Ann and I eventually parted ways, but she, her family, and that beautiful ramp changed my life forever.

I SPENT THE FIRST TEN years of my life in a wheelchair thinking no woman would ever want to have a romantic relationship with someone in a situation such as mine—much less that her family would accept it.

I was wrong.

To My Caregivers:
Thank you from the bottom of my heart!

Pete	Alicia	Lisa	Maria	Jenna	Gabbie
Chris	Aimee	Kelly	Geney	Brittney	Jordan(2)
Ryan	Sarah	Jennifer	Precious(2)	Elijah	Desiree
Mark	Denise	Silka	Maria(2)	Kristen(2)	Vanessa
Dan	Sam	Evi	Tim	Alex	Bree
Jeff	Lindsey	Liz	Sarah(2)	Alison	Ashley
Chad	Ellen	Kamila	Laura	Angie(2)	Kalina
Jim	Gwon	Shannon	Lara	Angela	Tammy
Jeff(2)	Joe	Erica	Marisa	Hyeran	Michaela(2)
Brett	Melissa	Mary Kate	Chloe	Jordan	Alyssa
Josh	Carrie	Kaitrin	Melanie	Julie(2)	Brenda
Chad	Ann	Kristen	Micah	Michaela	Amber
Dave	Britta	Emily	Julie	Erica(2)	Jenni
Dan(2)	Erin	Erin	Elisabeth	Nicole	Danielle
Andy	Jodi	Jaclyn	Anna	Jake	Mackenzie
Sean	Carrie(2)	Ann(2)	Fana	Elliot	Laura(2)
Suzanne	Angie	Valerie	Marisa(2)	Samantha	Victoria
Dogna	Deb	Precious	Caroline	Tara	Katie(2)
Alissa	David	Danny	Sarah(3)	Ryan	John
Terry	Austin	Pete(2)	Kateri	Jessica	Taylor
Katie	Amanda	Cailin	Stephanie	Anjana	

*The list starts in January of 1992 at the first name (Pete) and goes down, then up to the next row (Alicia), then down again, etc. The numbers represent the order of caregivers with the same name. For example, I've had three people named Sarah help me.

Tip #5
It's Time to Demonstrate Your Character

"WHERE'S YOUR HANDICAPPED TAG? Show me your handicapped tag!" yelled the gray-haired woman, banging on my driver-side window.

I'd just pulled into a disabled parking spot at a grocery store in Hyattsville, Maryland, a few blocks across the Northeast D.C. border. She was in her late sixties, many years of which were undoubtedly unfair to her, likely fueling her pessimism and igniting the fire behind her scorching glare.

"What?" I muddled, shocked by this explosion of anger before me.

"You can't park here without a handicapped tag! Where's your tag?"

"It's right there," I motioned to my dashboard, trying to point with my withered, paralyzed fist.

"Where? I don't see it!"

"Right there!" I barked back, my indignation growing.

"It's supposed to be hanging from your rearview mirror!"

"I don't have a rearview mirror!" I responded. (We were both yelling now.)

"It's supposed to be visible! Where is it? This parking space is for the handicapped!"

She walked around to the front of my van, searching for my parking tag. Upon seeing it, her glare only narrowed, its intensity undiminished. She stopped, scowled at me harshly, and then walked back to her car.

She was parked directly behind me. But rather than drive away, she backed up to wait for me to get out of my van. It seemed my little blue plastic parking tag didn't convince her in the slightest I was qualified to park there.

Seeing her waiting, I took my sweet ginger time unlocking my wheelchair from its driving position and rolling to the back of the van where my wheelchair lift was located (hence there being no need for a rearview mirror—I couldn't see out the back anyway).

After the automatic doors swung open and my wheelchair lift unfolded, I quickly rolled out onto the platform and turned my gaze toward my skeptical friend. Bearing down on her, I didn't need to try to imagine what was running through her mind—her blanched face said it all. She was a dark-skinned black woman, and upon seeing my wheelchair, her complexion went pale-white. David Duke looked black by comparison.

There was no question whether I was qualified to park there. I knew it, and upon seeing my wheelchair, she knew it, too. Yet if the fire in her eyes extinguished, I'll never know. Rather than driving forward past me, she quickly turned her head and put her car in reverse—not even using her own rearview mirror to back up. I never saw her again.

ONE OF THE REALITIES (dare I say: benefits) of being in a wheelchair is that you receive instant credibility. People simply can't help but recognize you're facing a difficult challenge. And when they see you out and about trying your best to live a normal life despite your challenge, you often gain their respect without even saying a word.

Sitting at home crying about your challenge is an option others can see you've decided not to choose. They wonder if they would be at home doing just that if they were in your situation. "Thank God that's not me," they might think to themselves. Of course in the recesses of their minds, they want to believe that if the roles were reversed, they'd be strong enough to handle it in the same way you are. But they can't know for sure.

What is for sure is the fact you're sitting right there in front of them, not quitting at all. Instead, you're thumbing your nose at this Goliath-sized challenge. This helps put their own problems in perspective, as well as to illuminate the power, resiliency, and beauty of the human spirit.

They use words such as "courageous," "brave," "inspirational," and "hero" to describe you. You don't totally feel comfortable being labeled as such, but that doesn't mean you don't like hearing these compliments.

If they're hip to the latest politically correct vernacular, they'll stay away from calling you *handicapped*—an antiquated term, which some people in wheelchairs find offensive. "I'm handi-*capable*, not handicapped," you'll hear from the mouths of a few angry disabled people. But be careful, for as soon as you call them disabled, they'll respond, "I'm making a disability a possibility, thank you very much." Similarly, *wheelchair-bound* fails, as people do get out of their chairs often, and it speculates as to their unfortunate (albeit likely accurate) future. And don't even try *differently abled*—that's just plain stupid and never caught on. So you really don't know what the hell to call me and my people. I know all this because one of my favorite things to do when I first meet certain people is to catch them in these very traps just to mess with their heads. They're usually friends of friends who I know can handle a little bit of a hard time. But having only just met me, they don't know if I'm kidding or if I'm serious. It's a lot of fun . . . at least for me.

But irrespective of whatever labels or terms are thrown around, when you're sitting there in a wheelchair, it's clear to everyone you're facing one of life's challenges. It's as recognizable as the bald head of a child with cancer or the red band at the tip of a blind person's white cane. It's overt, obvious, and in your face. Only on the subway in New York City does a wheelchair have no meaning at all. Riding around there in an $8,000 electric wheelchair is just a ploy to get the big $1.00 off a subway ticket.

"Do you really think I'm down here in a wheelchair just to get $1.00 off my ticket?" I've asked many an MTA employee behind the glass when they refuse to give me the disabled discount.

"Do you have a Medicare card?" they respond lamely, then add, "I don't make the rules," conceding they're not smart enough to think outside the rules. "We can only give the disabled discount if you have a Medicare card."

New York subways notwithstanding, being in a wheelchair is a lot like the old American Express slogan: membership has its privileges. And this isn't limited to good parking, cutting-in on long lines, having bigger bathroom stalls, and discounts. No, although those perks are nice, maybe the greatest privilege or benefit of being in a wheelchair is the lack of a need to explain or justify the challenge you're facing in life. Everyone can just see it.

This privilege, however, is unknown to people struggling with the countless other challenges beneath the surface—things like depression, back pain, neck pain, addiction, migraines, chronic arthritis, eating disorders, and extreme anxiety, just to name a few. My heart goes out to people facing challenges such as these. For these people, the suffering is internal. It's hidden. It's a secret.

People who face challenges that aren't obvious to the eye are left with two choices: struggle silently or admit to their plight and open themselves up to the scrutiny and judgment of others. If they choose the latter, they are stuck explaining and defending the magnitude, severity, and impact of their complication—not to mention dealing with the complication itself. It's hard enough to deal with a serious challenge in life, but even harder if you feel the need to constantly clarify and justify the challenge.

So it only stands to reason that at certain times—if only for the briefest and most fleeting of moments—these people find themselves wishing they had the benefit of instant credibility from an obvious impediment, such as being in a wheelchair. Not that they'd necessarily trade places. But it must be exhausting to feel the need to balance saying too much or too little about their challenge, while at the same time needing to confront it.

In the end, however, it makes no difference whether an obstacle is external or internal, obvious or hidden, loud or silent. Either way, your credibility is on the line. That's right: your challenge is calling you out.

Everyone knows it's easy to consider yourself a strong person when everything is going your way. Having a positive outlook on life isn't too tough after just being told you won Select-Five in the Powerball. Whistling "Zippity Doo Dah" and blowing sunshine up everyone's keister is easy when you're not facing any difficulties in your life.

But how about when things get tough? How about when everything *is not* going your way? Because that's when the rubber hits the road. And that, my friend, is when you demonstrate your character.

Former NFL star quarterback, Brett Favre, had an amazing career with the Green Bay Packers. (He then became a quarterback for the Minnesota Vikings, blew a chance for them to go to the Super Bowl by throwing an interception instead of easily running untouched for ten yards, and "allegedly" texted a picture of his tube steak to a trainer.) In a 2007 *Sports Illustrated* article, after having received the Sportsman of the Year award, Favre was asked of his favorite memory from his many years of playing football. The article provides that,

> [Favre] is quiet for a moment. "I've got so many plays running through my mind," he says, finally. "The funny thing is, it's not only about the touchdowns and the big victories. If I were to make a list, I would include the interceptions, the sacks, the really painful losses. Those times when I've

been down, when I've been kicked around, I hold on to those. In a way those are the best times I've ever had, because that's when I've found out who I am. And what I want to be."

I've never texted a picture of my tallywacker to anyone, but I'm pretty sure Favre nailed it there with his quote. You've been given a choice. You can complain. You can wallow in your own misery. You can play the victim. And you can cry "woe is me" until the cows come home.

Or you can accept that now is your time to showcase your strength. Now is your time to underscore that when the chips are down, you're not a quitter. You're a fighter. Now is when you demonstrate who you are and what you want to be.

And when you make it through to the other side of this—and you *will* make it through—it's at that point you'll know you've earned the credibility to hold your head high. You'll be proud of how you handled yourself then and how you're handling yourself now. And your strength of character will be evident for all to see—most importantly, by you.

Chapter Twelve

Washington

WHEN KAREN WAS A PATIENT at George Washington University Hospital in Washington, D.C., she became good friends with one of her nurses. Jane was a year or two younger than Karen and had graduated from Georgetown University with a degree in nursing. Being rather creative with nicknames, we called her "Jane the Nurse." And although Jane the Nurse had only been out of college for a year and, therefore, wasn't exactly "well-seasoned" in the field of nursing, she exuded such an obvious confidence (read: cockiness) about her own abilities that we liked her right away.

When Karen was out of the hospital between treatments (when she wasn't back in Pensacola with the Juder) she would stay with Jane in the house Jane rented with some friends, and Jane the Nurse would take care of her. Looking back on it, I'm sure Jane was breaking some sort of rule, or at least was discouraged by her colleagues from continuing to do as she did. But Jane did as Jane wanted.

One of the great silver linings of Karen's cancer was that she eventually broke up with her loser boyfriend. After spending much of her time consoling him and making sure he was handling her fight with cancer well, she bought him a plane ticket and shipped his sorry ass back to whatever rock he'd climbed out from under.

With Karen newly single, it became a running joke in the hospital that we were looking for a new boyfriend for her. We playfully interrogated all the doctors and nurses for any potential suitors for Karen. Characteristically eager to provide the solution, Jane the Nurse chimed in with the availability of her two single brothers. One brother had dark hair, the other, fire-engine-red.

"We're beach people, Jane," I was quick to inform her. "The last thing we need is some pasty-white redhead who can't stay in the sun for very long. We'll go with the dark-haired brother."

And so the joke continued with Jane the Nurse month after month as Karen continued her fight with leukemia.

When Karen was eventually discharged from George Washington Hospital and deemed cancer-free, she lived with Jane and her friends for several months. Jane continued to monitor Karen's health as she convalesced, and Karen periodically went back to GW for check-ups.

After a while, however, Karen needed to move on with her life. It had been a few months since she'd seen the Juder at my graduation from Saint Ben's/Saint John's, so she decided to head home to Pensacola. Jane, of course, offered to drive with Karen as she returned to Pensacola with a car full of all her stuff. Karen's plan was to live with the Juder for the summer before moving to Atlanta in the fall. It turned out that the financial aid forms the Juder filled out the night before Karen was to die proved successful—Karen was heading to Emory University in September to begin a master's in hospital administration.

As part of their trip to Pensacola, Jane asked if it'd be okay if they drove over to New Orleans one night. New Orleans is less than a three-hour drive from Pensacola, and her brother Matt lived there. He had graduated from Tulane University in New Orleans and still lived in the area. He was the same age as Karen and had flaming red hair.

Karen agreed to the trip and they drove over from Pensacola one day. That evening, they went out to a bar to take in some of the New Orleans nightlife. To hear Jane tell the story, when she heard Matt compliment Karen on one of her rings, she thought, "When has Matt ever even noticed a ring on a girl, much less thought to compliment her on it?"

Karen and Matt danced together all night long. As cliché as it sounds, they felt it was love at first sight—something genuinely out of a fairy tale.

Jane and Karen returned to Pensacola the next day, and Karen and Matt's magical night of dancing segued into talking on the phone regularly and plotting their next chance to see each other.

Not long after, Karen left for a trip to Barbados with some of her friends from Washington. It was somewhat of a "Celebrate Life" trip they organized while she was still in the hospital. The plan was for Karen to fly from Pensacola to Washington, layover for a few days for a quick checkup at GW, then meet her friends in Barbados for the celebration.

After being in remission for over six months, the results of her checkups were quite predictable. As always, the results of the blood tests came back quickly. More good news, then off to the Caribbean, Karen expected. This time, however, the results were different. Her cancer had returned. She was dying again. A bone marrow transplant was necessary in order for her to survive. Chemotherapy had failed.

Naturally, Jane the Nurse was with Karen to shoulder this news, and to hear that her friend was now looking at a fifty-fifty probability of surviving. It was devastating. And to complicate matters, someone had to call Matt to tell him.

Yet even that was more difficult than it appeared. The problem was that Jane had never told Matt how she became friends with Karen. She never told him Karen had been one of her patients. Matt had no idea when he met Karen that she'd just survived a fight with cancer. He thought her short haircut was just the new style. He was completely in the dark about all of it.

Jane never discussed it with Matt because she felt it should be Karen's decision who and when she told of her fight with cancer. And Karen wasn't exactly trying to keep it a big secret from Matt the night they met. It's just, how often do you introduce yourself with your name and list of your ailments?

There were certainly opportunities for Karen to tell Matt about it during their many phone conversations, but why not wait to discuss it in person? Besides, it's safe to say Karen felt a fair amount of trepidation in telling the person she just met, and had feelings for, that she had serious medical issues.

So, Karen and Jane decided it was best to have Jane call Matt to deliver the bad news. Having Karen call would have put way too much pressure on Matt. The simple truth was that Karen and Matt barely knew each other. They had only seen each other once. And the road ahead for Karen was completely uncertain. Matt deserved the opportunity to bow out gracefully. This was not something he signed up for. Quite to the contrary, this was something actually kept from him.

Matt listened intently as Jane described Karen's situation—the past, present, and troubled future. She did not hold back in painting every possible outcome, with heavy emphasis on the worst case scenario. Karen would be in the hospital for months, during most of which she'd be in extreme isolation in the bone marrow transplant unit. She'd lose her hair again. She'd constantly be fighting infections. She'd be completely debilitated with nausea and would vomit regularly. And at the end of all this, Jane candidly told Matt, there was a significant possibility that Karen would die.

Silence followed. Total silence. Nothing but a long, difficult, and absolute silence.

In many respects, Karen had been fighting for her life for close to a year at that point. Yet in a just a few short moments, Matt was thrust into a world he was not prepared for. What could he possibly say? His response was silence.

It's actually quite rare, really, to be able to maintain silence in a conversation for very long, especially when it seems there are so many questions to be asked. The silence is uncomfortable, so we speak—often before we think. Or we speak to help us think. Or we speak and never think.

But Matt was silent.

Eventually, Jane had to ask her brother how he'd like to handle this. Despite his initial silence, Matt's reply to Jane was immediate, and both firm and reflective—his measured words equal parts resolute and likely a bit startling to him, through its own self-realization:

"I've spent my whole life trying to find someone like her," Matt stated clearly. "I don't plan to lose her now."

From that moment on, Matt never wavered.

Too often when couples first start dating, there's a lot of game-playing and strategizing. "Should I text today or should I wait a day?" "Should I say how I feel, or should I wait until they tell me first?" There was none of that with Matt.

Karen still went on her trip to Barbados with her friends. She then returned to Pensacola for a few days before heading back to Washington to enter the hospital. Matt drove over from New Orleans to visit her. They went camping for a night on Dauphin Island in Alabama. And because I'm her brother, let's assume they played cards most of the night and then retired to separate sleeping bags.

Once Karen was back in the hospital, Matt called every single day, visited Washington as often as he could, and provided her with every reason to fight vehemently through all she was facing.

During one of his visits to Washington, Matt was alone with Karen in the bone marrow transplant unit. (Karen ultimately received a transplant of her own bone marrow—called an autologous bone transplant—where they took out her own bone marrow, purified it, and then put it back into her body.) She was completely bald at the time and had a horrific rash on her head and face as a result of an allergic reaction to a medication. She had vomited a few times that day and generally felt like ass warmed over. It was a bad day.

In the midst of all this, Matt was overcome with emotion and couldn't wait any longer for what he wanted to do. He grabbed Karen's hand and dropped down on one knee beside her hospital bed. He told her how much he loved her and that he wanted to marry her.

"Will you marry me?" he asked her.

Karen cried, of course, and admitted that she was in love with him, too. She told Matt she had been wanting to say it to him for some time, but he beat her to it. Yet despite her feelings, she felt she couldn't say yes to him. At least not at that moment.

"Let's make sure I don't die first," she said to him, reluctantly and painfully, turning down his proposal. "If I don't die, I hope you ask me again when I'm out of the hospital."

So they left it there.

Karen was eventually released from GW Hospital. About ten months after that, she and Matt were married in Pensacola. Matt asked her to marry him again almost as soon as she walked out the hospital doors. This time, she said yes.

They married in mid-October 1995, two months after Hurricane Erin rolled through Pensacola and did a fair amount of damage, and about ten days after Hurricane Opal destroyed much of Pensacola Beach, throwing many of their wedding plans to the wind (literally). Of course none of that fazed Matt and Karen in the slightest—they'd already weathered much stronger storms.

I was a groomsman and Jane the Nurse was the maid of honor. Matt and Karen now have three children, are happily married, and live in Newtown, Pennsylvania. Karen remains cancer-free.

And as luck would have it, Matt is able to stay in the sun for long periods of time. Thank you, SPF-90 sunblock!

AFTER CLOSE TO FOUR YEARS of working in the Division of Corporation Finance at the U.S. Securities and Exchange Commission in Washington, I left to pursue the bright lights of the big city. (New York, New York.)

During my first two years of living in Washington, I wasn't sure if I'd ever leave. Working for the government provided me with an amazing quality of life. I didn't have to bill clients for every minute of my time. The hours were predictable, reasonable, and fairly stress free. The salary was surprisingly quite good. My colleagues were awesome. And there was the underlying feeling of public service that I greatly enjoyed.

Yet part of me also became disenchanted with how I was spending each day of my working life. In certain aspects of government work, there's a lack of meritocracy and accountability. Promotion and seniority sometimes hinges simply on the number of years spent showing up. And there were times when it seemed not to matter how well or how poorly a job was done—it simply needed to get done.

That's certainly not to say I can't name friends and former colleagues working at the SEC who are incredible public servants. I was fortunate enough to work with many extraordinarily intelligent people who could make ten times their SEC salary if they went to the private sector. But I didn't feel connected to the work in the ways these people did. I began feeling semiretired—all I needed to do was show up for work the next thirty-five years, and then I'd be officially retired. Despite good intentions, I lacked the discipline to keep working hard at that job; I found myself slacking quite a bit.

That being said, the depth of knowledge in securities law I gained there was essentially a golden ticket. It was hard enough to land a well-paying job in New York City, but even harder to pull a Sully Sullenberger soft landing at an elite Wall Street law firm.

I left the SEC for the Big Apple secure with a job and a fat salary at Clifford Chance, which, at the time, was the largest law firm on the whole planet, based on revenues.

Life is full of unexpected surprises. Who knew the boy from Pensacola who could barely get into college would one day be a Wall Street lawyer? Certainly not my grade school and high school teachers. And it certainly would have never turned out this way if not for a bit of focus and discipline thrust upon me by a broken neck.

Take the good with the bad, baby. You really have no other choice.

BEFORE HEADING TO WALL STREET, however, it was time to see more of the world. Shortly after leaving the SEC, I boarded a plane. Destination: the Netherlands, Turkey, Georgia, Azerbaijan, Turkmenistan, Uzbekistan, Kazakhstan, Mongolia, China, and Russia.

Life is also full of excitement, especially when you decide to make it exciting. Many of the extraordinary things that have happened in my life—including plenty of unexpected surprises—did not happen completely by chance. In fact, you'd be hard-pressed to come up with examples of many people who have led extraordinary lives merely as a result of chance. To the contrary, ensuring a life chock-full of excitement requires a conscious, purposeful, and persistent pursuit of exhilarating experiences.

Life truly is what you make of it.

Tip #6
There's Strength in Numbers

THINKING OF THIS LITTLE vignette may help at certain times:

When looking to God for the answer to "Why me?" imagine the clouds parting, a warm bright light shining down on you, birds chirping, a golden harp playing, and the feeling of peace. You take a deep breath and allow this wonderful feeling to settle in. Just then, however, a LOUD and very annoyed voice comes booming down from the heavens. The answer to your question has arrived. His response to you is simply pointing out the obvious: "IT'S NOT JUST YOU, YOU SELF-ABSORBED ASSHOLE!"

The not-so-subtle point is that whenever you think it's *just* you, that you're alone in your struggles, that no one has endured or will ever endure something as bad as you, then you've lost perspective.

Take comfort in knowing that you're not the first, you're not alone, and you won't be the last to face one of life's challenges. You can and will make it through this.

Welcome to the club!

SPINAL CORD INJURY—Approximately 288,000 people live with spinal cord injuries, and nearly 11,000 people receive spinal cord injuries each year.

DIVORCE—Approximately forty to fifty percent of marriages end in divorce.

CANCER—Nearly 12 million people are living with cancer. Approximately 1.6 million new cases are diagnosed each year, and approximately 600,000 die each year from cancer.

DIABETES—Nearly 25.8 million people have diabetes.

SUICIDE—An estimated 730,000 attempts are made and approximately 35,000 people commit suicide each year.

CEREBRAL PALSY—Approximately 764,000 people manifest one or more of the symptoms of cerebral palsy.

BRAIN INJURY—At least 5.3 million people have permanent brain injuries, 1.4 million sustain an injury each year, and 50,000 die.

STUBBED TOE—Every year millions of barefoot people stub their toe walking and say it hurts like a bitch. People in wheelchairs just roll by and laugh their asses off when they see it happen.

HEART DISEASE—Close to 13 million people live with heart disease, and over 695,000 die each year.

BANKRUPTCY—Nearly 1.46 million individuals declare bankruptcy each year.

INTELLECTUAL DISABILITY—An estimated 7.2 million people have intellectual disabilities (formerly known as mental retardation) and related developmental disabilities.

ALCOHOL AND DRUG ADDICTION—Approximately 23.5 million people are addicted to alcohol and drugs. Two million suffer from alcohol-related liver disease. One hundred die from overdose each day.

BURN VICTIM—Up to 2.4 million burn injuries are reported per year, and between 8,000 and 12,000 people die of burns each year.

DOWN'S SYNDROME—Approximately 350,000 people have Down's Syndrome, and 5,000 children are born with it each year.

TEEN PREGNANCY—About 330,000 teenagers give birth each year, and many more become pregnant.

PARKINSON'S DISEASE—An estimated 1.5 million people currently have Parkinson's disease, and 60,000 new cases are diagnosed each year.

SCHIZOPHRENIA—Approximately 2.7 million people are afflicted by schizophrenia. No, they aren't. Yes, they are.

MULTIPLE SCLEROSIS—About 400,000 people have MS, and nearly 200 more people are diagnosed each week.

MUSCULAR DYSTROPHY—Nearly 250,000 people have muscular dystrophy.

BLIND—I saw somewhere that approximately 1.3 million people are blind, and 50,000 more become blind each year.

SPINA BIFIDA—Approximately 70,000 people have spina bifida, and approximately eight babies are born with it every day.

DRUNK DRIVING—Nearly 17,000 people are killed in alcohol-related crashes, an average of one almost every half-hour.

AUTISM—Nearly 1.5 million people have autism, and it's found in one of every eighty-eight children.

RAPE—Approximately 90,000 women report being raped each year.

EPILEPSY—More than 2.7 million people are living with epilepsy, and 181,000 develop seizures and epilepsy every year.

PRISON—Nearly 2.3 million adults are incarcerated, and over 4.8 million are on probation or on parole. (Who doesn't love *The Shawshank Redemption*? "Get busy living, or get busy dying.")

DROWNING—Approximately 3,500 drownings occur each year, about ten each day.

TOXIC SHOCK SYNDROME—Colin Powell and Newt Gingrich seem convinced this will happen to most women on the battlefield.

MURDER—Approximately 14,000 people are murdered each year.

EATING DISORDER—Up to 24 million people suffer from an eating disorder (e.g., anorexia, bulimia, and binge-eating).

CAR ACCIDENT—Approximately 30,000 people die each year in car accidents.

AMPUTEE—Nearly 1.7 million people are living with limb loss.

MISCARRIAGE—Approximately one in four pregnancies ends in miscarriage; some estimates are as high as one in three.

UNEMPLOYMENT—About 11.7 million people are unemployed.

UNIVERSITY OF SAINT THOMAS—Approximately 10,300 students attend this lame school in Minnesota.

LUPUS—Almost 2 million people have lupus, or one person out of every 185.

DEAF—I heard somewhere that nearly 10 million people are hard of hearing and close to 1 million are functionally deaf.

DEATH—Over 2.4 million people died last year.

STROKE—Approximately 795,000 people suffer a stroke each year.

ALZHEIMER'S—Almost forgot: An estimated 4.5 million people have Alzheimer's. The number will grow to between 11.3 and 16 million by 2050.

*These numbers relate to the United States only. (Think of how much bigger they'd be including the rest of the world.) The source of all this information is the Internet, which is always accurate.

Chapter Thirteen

Mana Pools

I'VE SPENT TENS OF THOUSANDS of dollars over my lifetime on travel and I don't regret one penny of it—it's by far the best money I've ever spent.

As you get older and the years pass by (which is a bit redundant), the monotony of working, the steadiness of routine, and the tedium of life can produce essentially no definitive memories. It all seems to blend together. But embark on an adventure to a foreign land, even if only for a few days, and those vivid memories will be with you forever.

I was twenty-seven years old the first time I left the United States. I returned from that trip (and every trip since then) a slightly different person from when I left. My horizons are broadened and clearer. My appreciation for many aspects of my life are renewed or appreciated anew.

Unfailingly, the emphasis I placed on certain aspects of my life before the journey no longer seem worthy of such emphasis upon my return. Things that seemed right to me, or "as they should be," I unexpectedly have reason to question—the results of which enable me to hold such beliefs more firmly (having truly questioned their foundation), or become skeptical of them, or realize I was simply wrong about them.

Similarly, places and events I'd previously only read or heard about suddenly have context and greater interest to me after visiting them. (Passing through a West Bank check-point en route to Bethlehem, for example, under the stern and suspicious eyes of a young machine gun-toting soldier does a great deal to enlighten the complicated Israeli-Palestinian conflict.) Following these sojourns, I'm also able to join in on conversations I didn't feel part of previously. And at parties, I'm able to enthrall and regale throngs of adoring fans with tales of my adventures, and beautiful ladies regularly proffer themselves to me. (Okay, now I've traveled to Fantasy Island.) But I am more engaged in the world having left my comfort zone, and arguably more interesting to others.

The adventure I embarked on after leaving the SEC was actually the third time I'd left America the Beautiful.

My first overseas experience occurred while working at Arthur Andersen in Minneapolis. I built up enough vacation to take a month off and used it to travel through Europe. I landed in Paris with my caregiver, Sam, a Johnnie who had graduated the same year as me. I didn't know Sam in college, but he began helping me as a caregiver while working toward being admitted to medical school.

I could tell within the first fifteen minutes that Sam was completely overwhelmed. It's one thing to weather the frustrations of being in a wheelchair after building up years of metaphoric scar tissue. It's quite another to face these same frustrations unprotected.

Sam was an experienced traveler. He'd frequented Paris often while studying abroad in Cannes, France, and he'd popped around Western Europe a fair bit visiting most of its main attractions. Yet none of that prepared him for the obstacles and exasperations of foreign travel in a wheelchair. Sam's passport was stamped to enter France. When pushing my wheelchair, however, he quickly realized he'd crossed the border into a much more foreign land. It seemed like an entirely different planet. Simply making it across the street could be absurdly difficult. Climbing a flight of stairs was often next to impossible. (*Welcome to Planet Gimp,* Sam must have thought. *No passport required.*)

The year was 1997, and Gay Paree was extremely inaccessible for wheelchairs. There were no curb-cuts on the corners of any blocks. And stairs were virtually everywhere you looked—including a steep flight at the entrance of our hotel, which advertised as "wheelchair accessible." Even the doorway to enter our room at this hotel openly mocked any tenable definition of wheelchair accessibility. It was so narrow an emaciated crack addict would need to use an enema just to inch through it. I had lockers in high school with bigger doors. Sam was forced to pick me up and carry me like a new bride into our room. It was impossible to believe any wheelchair could fit through that sliver of a doorway. Not that there was any space for it, anyway, inside our tiny "wheelchair accessible" room.

Sam ultimately went on to receive a master's from Yale University and a Ph.D. from the University of Notre Dame . . . in *theology*. (I suspect he prayed to the good Lord so much during our traveling experience, he figured he might as well just keep going and get a few degrees for it.)

The great news is that I visited Paris again in 2012, and vast improvements had been made in their wheelchair accessibility. (Karen, Matt and their children lived in Lyon, France, for a few years for Matt's job.) I'd now dare say that someone in a wheelchair could live in Paris without undue frustration, by which I mean there are curb cuts on most corners, public transportation is largely accessible, and the overwhelming majority of business establishments are accessible. A truly wonderful example of how things change with time.

In addition to testing Sam's patience in France, we also traveled to Germany, the Czech Republic, Austria(where I flipped over in my chair but didn't split my head open due to marionettes from Prague in my backpack), Switzerland, and Italy (Jeff joined us in Florence). Backpacking in Europe is unquestionably an awesome way to cut your traveling teeth—whether in a wheelchair or not. We had a fantastic time meeting and drinking with the requisite number of Australians, Canadians, and Americans (who, in my experience, with the possible exception of Israelis, make up the largest group of hardcore travelers).

My second trip abroad was decidedly more ambitious than my first (or at least required more shots from a doctor, included a few hallucinations on malaria medication, and resulted in several more near-death experiences). I took this trip while working at the SEC, after once again accruing another month of vacation. This trip was to Mother Africa.

Greg, a phenomenal friend and another Johnnie who graduated alongside me, was working at the time for Catholic Relief Services in Harare, Zimbabwe. My caregiver, Emily, and I kicked off the trip by flying to London for a week to check it out. (London is a very wheel-chair accessible city.)

It was on the flight from Washington to London when I started thinking about how many pills I take each day for my muscle spasms. (Muscle spasms are a common side effect of a spinal cord injury.) Halfway across the Atlantic, it dawned on me that I'd only packed half the pills I needed for the month.

No big deal, I thought, *I'll just call my doctor in the States when we land and have him order more pills to a pharmacy in London.*

Wrong!

A U.S. doctor can only order prescriptions to U.S. pharmacies. When traveling abroad, there's a whole racket set up for foreign travel-ers in need of a prescription. It usually requires going to a hospital, where they'll charge an obscene fee to meet with a doctor for two min-utes and have him or her write the script. (Exactly what I ended up doing in London to obtain my pills.)

Finding a hospital in London, however, proved to be a tally-ho bit more difficult than we expected, especially considering Emily and I spoke American (oops, I mean English) pretty goodly.

Every person in Piccadilly Circus we asked for directions to the hospital kept telling us where to go for a surgery.

"Oh, you need a surgery?" they'd say to us in their Grey Poupon accent.

"What?" I'd respond, confused. "No, I don't need surgery, I just need to find a doctor to prescribe me some pills."

(It turns out the British call a hospital a *surgery*.)

If you're staying in a nice-enough hotel, however, you can avoid the hospital altogether. What you do instead is ask the front desk to bring a doctor to your room. This scenario happened to me in Portugal about a year ago when the airline lost all my bags for four days, following a one-hour flight from Casablanca, Morocco, to Lisbon, Portugal. The Portuguese doctor came to my hotel and charged me one hundred U.S. dollars for maybe thirty seconds of work.

But my trip to Zimbabwe made the hassle of surgeries in London well worth it. It was truly a once-in-a-lifetime experience. Jeff flew over to London and met Emily and I on our last day there. The three of us then took the ten-hour flight to Zimbabwe to begin a three-week trip.

My best story of Zimbabwe involves canoeing down the Zambezi River. (That's right: a quadriplegic canoeing down the African river separating Zimbabwe and Zambia.) Emily and a guide were in one canoe. Greg and Jeff were in another canoe, and I sat in the middle of a third canoe, with a guide in the back and our pilot in the front. We'd chartered a tiny plane to fly us "into the bush" of the Mana Pools National Park, Zimbabwe, where we slept in tents. On our first night there one of the guides suggested I bring my manual wheelchair into the tent with me.

"Why?" I asked incredulously. "Is an elephant gonna steal it?"

"No," he replied, very matter-of-factly. "But the hyenas will likely eat all the rubber off your tires." (Hmm . . . I hadn't thought of that.)

As we canoed down the Zambezi, it was important for each group to frequently bang the edge of their canoe with an oar. The Zambezi River has one of the highest hippo populations in the world. If you unexpectedly canoe over the top of a hippo and frighten it, causing it to pop its head up and flip your canoe over, it will likely maul you to death. (Who knew these fat bastards were so dangerous?)

Hippos aside, there was also a restrained concern about the countless number of crocodiles sunning themselves on the river's edges, many of which measured fourteen feet or longer.

At one point during our three-hour leisurely meandering down the Zambezi, Greg and Jeff were canoeing right beside my canoe. Amidst the calm water and tranquility of the surroundings, they suddenly started paddling backwards, splashing, and yelling.

"Gator! Gator!" they screamed.

Without warning, a large crocodile suddenly revealed itself between our two canoes. Not that I saw it, mind you—it's just the way Greg and Jeff were thrashing about (and the way the guide and pilot jerked my canoe), I believed them. All the commotion then caused me to lose my balance, which is why I fell to one side, and how my upper body ended up dangling halfway out of the canoe—over the same side as the crocodile.

"Quit leaning! Quit leaning!" shouted Daniel, the guide behind me, frantically.

"I'm not leaning!" I shouted back. "I lost my balance!"

With the left side of my body close to the water, I flailed my right arm desperately, trying to catch the side of the canoe with my wrist. My paralyzed hand and fingers were of no use to me. What I needed to do was hook the back of my wrist on the edge of the canoe, and then I knew I could pull my unresponsive torso straight. But I couldn't hook the damn edge, so I kept flailing. And Daniel kept screaming at me.

Eventually my spastic effort paid off. I hooked my wrist and was upright once again. But Daniel was clearly shaken up. For the rest of canoe trip, he was totally different. When we stopped briefly for lunch on a riverbank, he was nervous and constantly looking around. And once back on the river, he tried to hurry us along. Our leisurely drift turned into more of a race to the finish.

When the canoe trip was over and we were safely in the jeep heading back to our campsite, we discussed whether we should go back on the river later that afternoon. A cold beer on the Zambezi watching the lava-orange African sunset did sound pretty cool. But it was clear Daniel was completely against the idea.

A few minutes later, another jeep flagged us down and Daniel got out to talk to them.

"What was that all about?" I asked when he returned. He said nothing and started driving again. But I continued to prod.

"Well, if you must know," Daniel eventually answered reluctantly, "an American girl was killed on the river a few days ago."

"Shut up," I said, knowing full well he just didn't want to deal with bringing my broken body back out on the river.

"I'm serious," he said. "A crocodile rose up out of the river and bit her in half. Her sister was there and saw it. Her father was there and saw it, too. The park rangers ended up shooting a bunch of crocodiles and found the remains of her body inside them. She was sitting in the middle of the canoe when it happened."

Of course I didn't believe a word he said. Daniel was just being lazy. It was much easier for him if we stayed at our camp rather than dealing with the stress and hassle of getting me back on the river in a canoe. We were paying him good money, he just didn't want to earn it.

That being said, I was secretly sort of glad to get off that river. I knew from the day we started planning this trip that Greg and Jeff wanted to canoe down the Zambezi—and now we'd done it. It was exhilarating. Talk about feeling alive! And to go from living on a ventilator years earlier to canoeing down the freakin' Zambezi—it doesn't get any better than that!

But why push our luck? I thought. And so I was actually quite content sticking around the campsite that afternoon.

It was when I returned to Washington that I Googled Daniel's story to find out it was true. Katy Reeves from Spokane, Washington, was in fact killed by a crocodile days earlier on the Zambezi River. She is the only person included in my "Life Is Short—Make the Most of It" tip that I didn't actually know.

Katy was seventeen years old when she was killed. She was beautiful and had her whole life ahead of her. Why she was eaten by a crocodile and not me makes no sense. Why not spare her and take an older quadriplegic leaning over the side of the canoe?

Even while writing these words, I took a moment to speak to her, a young girl I never knew.

Quadriplegic canoeing down the Zambezi River.

Katy, I hope you feel that I've never taken my life for granted. I hope you feel I've done the best I could so far. Without a doubt I've had some good days and bad days, but I continue to try to make a difference with my life. I hope I've made you proud.

BEFORE MOVING FROM Washington to New York, I spent over twenty-five thousand dollars in two and a half months by traveling to ten countries. The trip went like this:

 ♿ I flew from D.C. to the Netherlands and spent several *hazy* days in Amsterdam;

 ♿ I flew from Amsterdam to Turkey and then traveled by bus (spending time in Istanbul, Ankara, Samsun, and Trabzon) into Georgia;

 ♿ I traveled by bus into Georgia (spending time in Tbilisi) and then by train into Azerbaijan;

 ♿ I traveled by train and car in Azerbaijan (spending time in Baku) and then took a ferryboat across the Caspian Sea into Turkmenistan;

 ♿ I flew twice in Turkmenistan (spending time in Turkmenbasi and Ashgabat) and then rolled my wheelchair across a bizarre one-hundred-dred-yard no-mans-land border separating Turkmenistan and Uzbekistan;

 ♿ I traveled in Uzbekistan by van (spending time in Urgench, Khiva, Bukhara, Samarkand, and Tashkent) and then flew to Kazakhstan;

 ♿ I traveled by train in Kazakhstan (spending time in Almaty) and then into China;

 ♿ I traveled by train completely across China—east to west (spending time in Urumqi, Xi'an, Luoyang, and Beijing)—and then flew to Mongolia (where I became a magician with my pants);

 ♿ I traveled by train in Mongolia (spending time in Ulaanbaatar) and then into Russia;

♿ I traveled by train in Russia (spending time in Irkutsk, Yekaterinburg, Moscow, and St. Petersburg) and then flew back to the Netherlands;

♿ I traveled in the metaphysical sense for one more night in Amsterdam, and then flew back to D.C.

Why did it cost me so much ($25,000) for only two and a half months? Well, although there's no shortage of travel guides with tips to help people in wheelchairs, my opinion is that traveling in a wheelchair really comes down to just one tip: bring some strong backs with you.

The world is not a wheelchair accessible place. The stairs you'll need to ascend and descend are countless. The miles of wretched cobblestone and thick sand you must traverse are vast. The variety of cars, vans, buses, Tok Toks, trains, planes, boats, canoes, carriages, and parasailing harnesses you'll eagerly (and reluctantly) get into and out of are limitless. And in way too many international hotels, what qualifies as "wheelchair accessible" means there's a place in the back to park your wheelchair, but then you'll need to climb up a flight of stairs, past the broken elevator that's too small to hold an injured Malibu Barbie, and through the attenuated door, next to the pile of enemas.

I paid for three strong backs to accompany me on this long trip. If I'd only paid for myself, it would have cost me about seven thousand bucks, but I paid all the expenses for two

Realizing the Great Wall might fail ADA code for "wheelchair accessibility," with Jeff in Beijing, China.

caregivers, Danny and Pete, and most of the expenses for Jeff, who quit his job as a drug-and-alcohol counselor to help me drink vast quantities of alcohol on the trip.

Danny and Pete were in between their junior and senior years at Catholic University in D.C. They lived with me as my caregivers the previous year and had strong backs, were willing to rough it quite a bit, and were perfectly content to work in exchange for traveling.

And while this trip was longer in duration and covered more ground than my prior two trips abroad, it presented many of the same type of frustrations I experienced on those trips—frustrations common to every international trip I've ever taken.

As much as I love traveling, it puts me in an unlimited number of scenarios that cause me to scratch my head and wonder why the hell I ever agreed to go on this dang trip, much less painstakingly plan it, and then heavily finance it.

Of course there are the typical things everyone experiences when traveling: being lost, tired, uncomfortable, hungry, worried, unable to speak or understand the language. Enduring these kinds of frustrations teaches you not only a lot about yourself, but more importantly, it teaches you incalculable amounts about your travel companions. As the saying goes, "Never marry someone until you've traveled with them." (And I suggest you add to that, "Never marry someone who doesn't like to travel.")

For a person traveling in a wheelchair, however, the experience entails a whole other layer of frustration—and is magnified tenfold if they're used to being rather independent.

By using an electric wheelchair in my normal, day-to-day life, I easily whip around, coming and going as I please. But when traveling internationally, using a manual wheelchair is really the only way to do it. Sure, you can pull off a trip in an electric wheelchair to a select number of cities in Europe: London, Paris, Munich, and Barcelona, to name a few. But you'd still be excluded from many restaurants, bars, and tourist sites by doing so. You'd also likely be forced to stay in the most expensive hotels to ensure true "wheelchair accessibility." Otherwise, using a manual wheelchair is the only option internationally.

Traveling domestically (in the U.S.) in an electric wheelchair has made great strides over the years. But the challenge of getting from the airport to your hotel, or anywhere after that, remains quite profound. Wheelchair accessible taxis are often hard to find (if available at all). And keep in mind that electric wheelchairs are freakin' heavy—mine weighs close to 300 pounds. So there's no way to pick it up to put it inside a regular taxi, or lift it over even one stair at someone's house, or at a restaurant, or a bar. Besides, it's much easier to break an electric wheelchair during a flight. So again, using a manual wheelchair is the frontrunner when traveling domestically.

The upside of traveling in a manual wheelchair is that it allows you to easily handle stairs, transfer in and out of cars, and have your wheelchair put in the trunk. (Never put your wheelchair in a separate car— it always rides with you! And if the trunk won't close, you need to put it in the backseat, even when the driver tells you, "It's okay. It won't fall out.")

The downside, however, is that someone is usually pushing your chair, and you're suddenly at the mercy of his or her driving skills. You feel the pain of every bump and pothole they hit—even though you often saw it coming. And you become responsible and feel the need to apologize when *they* run over someone's toes, or clip the heels of a stranger with your chair—even though it wasn't your fault.

There's also the increased risk of being injured. You're being tipped back, carried over, and rolled through a myriad of obstacles you never imagined, all of which present the dreadful possibility of you being dropped or flipped over—in which case your cute, little, soft head may be smashed open.

Keeping your wheelie bars down is unfortunately usually not an option, either—especially when traveling internationally, since someone is constantly tipping you back to make it over a curb or to go up or down stairs. Flipping the wheelie bars up and down each time is just too big of a hassle. So they stay up.

All these hazards and irritations are then compounded by the clear risk of your wheelchair being damaged from this rough travel. If that happens, you're totally hosed. Your best option internationally is to find a garage or bike shop and hope the people working there are smart, nice, and, most importantly, innovative. (The fix is unlikely to be straightforward.)

But wait, there's more.

You're also subject to the whims of whoever is pushing your manual wheelchair. If he or she wants to veer over and see something in a store, you veer over. If he or she wants to stop and take a picture, you stop. Contrast that with what *you* want when you're being pushed. You must *ask* to veer over to check out whatever it is that just caught your eye, or *ask* to stop for that perfect photo. Hell, you even need to *ask* to go to the bathroom because you need their help pushing you there. These frustrations wear on you.

All the while, you must try not to think about how disgustingly dirty you usually are. Through the act of pushing your manual wheelchair, you're basically walking around the streets of this foreign country on your hands. Your morbid mitts are black with funk and have stained your pants forever through the constant need to adjust your legs, which are being bounced to hell and back from the prehistoric terrain.

And when you arrive at that elusive restaurant, famished and ready to eat, don't for one minute think the bathroom will be wheelchair accessible and you'll be able to wash up. Not a chance. Your only consolation is to pour pounds of Purell over your grotesque paws and then try to avoid looking at that gnarly black scooty-juice under your nails as you take the next bite of whatever inedible intestines you're eating. (Yes, it turns out they didn't have a menu in English—you have no idea what you ordered.)

Of course the saving grace of all of this is something appreciated by every hardcore traveler: returning to the hotel after a long, hot, sweaty, frustrating day of traveling and savoring a soothing, steamy shower which feels so fantastic. That is, it feels that way to everyone who's not in a wheelchair. You can't fit in that bathroom, you gimp! What in tarnations are you thinking? At best you can *ask* (that's right: once again, freakin' *ask*!) your caregiver to help you wash up by using one of the two towels included in the room (a frustration that can't even be put into words). And don't bother going to the front desk to ask someone for some washcloths. Washcloths are basically an American thing. The rest of the world washes their ass with the same hand you just shook—if they wash their ass at all. Besides, you don't know how to pronounce *washcloth* in whatever language they speak in whatever country you're traveling in, anyway.

"SO WHY NOT STOP traveling when it obviously leads to so much frustration?" you may be asking. Well, I often ask myself that very question.

After being home from a trip for a short period of time, however, the answer always comes to me clearly: I quickly forget the frustrations and only remember the awesome experience—which I relive over and over.

I can close my eyes right now and think of a few sunsets that by themselves make all the money and hassle seem worth it. I've also witnessed breathtaking meadows, lakes, rivers, mountains, beaches, deserts, and skies that seemed too unbelievable to be real.

I've eaten amazing meals (both expected and unexpected) and had plenty of crappy ones that taught me a lesson.

Traveling has also put me in the position to witness much of the best of what human nature has to offer. No trip replete with adventure is possible without the help of countless strangers taking time to assist with directions, recommendations, and sage precautions. No trip of any great distance is possible without observing happy, thankful, fulfilled individuals, living life with much less than you. And few experiences can put a huge smile on your face as quickly, easily, and genuinely as where you witness the innocence of a child waving at your passing train, or carry on a conversation with someone so sincerely excited to meet you.

These are but a few of the wonderful benefits of traveling, and in truth, they avail themselves to anyone who travels. Ironically, however, when traveling in a wheelchair, there exists an opportunity for the whole experience to be even more special.

Without avoiding the obvious, I'll readily admit that my wheelchair has allowed me to move to the front of the line in so many airports and tourist attractions that I've sadly grown to somewhat expect it. Similarly, I've been bumped up to first class on many flights and been charged no fee or a reduced fee, and given VIP treatment at museums, churches, mosques, bars, restaurants, and major tourist sites the world over.

And while these perks are certainly wonderful, they are not what leave me shaking my head in disbelief and amazement as I relish a past traveling experience in a wheelchair, or look forward to the next. Instead, it is the people who have gone out of their way to help me surmount the seemingly limitless insurmountable obstacles of traveling the world in a wheelchair which have made my adventures so special. I've put my trust and safety into the hands (literally) of countless people over the years, many of whom were complete strangers. I asked plenty of these people to help me, and many more simply saw someone in need of assistance and did whatever they could to help.

At this point, I think Jeff has even forgotten how much easier it is to travel without the hassles of a wheelchair. But if you ask him, that type of traveling is devoid of the satisfaction of looking at the challenge presented by the next indomitable obstacle and saying to it, "Fuck you! We're gonna do this damn thing anyway!"

Fortunately for me, so many other family, friends, caregivers, and strangers have held this same attitude. Together, we've pulled off some of the craziest shit that no one expected a quadriplegic could ever do. It's been an awesome ride so far!

Chapter Fourteen

Ashgabat

PEOPLE OFTEN ASK ME what the best place I have visited is. With thirty-eight countries (and hundreds of cities) under my belt, my top five are as follows:

  ♿ VIETNAM. When looking for one country that can offer pretty much everything, Vietnam is it.

First of all, by landing in Ho Chi Minh City (HCMC, formerly Saigon) you're guaranteed a very unique and kickass big-city experience. The Paris of the Orient is a totally metropolitan city teeming with motorbikes—we're talking *waves* upon *waves* of people on motorbikes flooding the city streets. And it provides every type of restaurant, hotel, and shopping you could desire, complete with all the ranges of quality and price you want.

Second is its fascinating history. Because of the war in Vietnam, there are tons of impactful historical sites to check out around HCMC. The War Atrocities Museum, for example, shows some of the most grotesque and disturbing images of war you'll ever want to see. (They conveniently only feature atrocities committed by U.S. solders against the Vietnamese.) Similarly, the Cu Chi Tunnels tour is close by, where you can see the types of underground tunnels the Vietnamese used in the war, as well as some of the completely effed-up booby-traps they utilized. My favorite part of the tour was at the beginning when they played a video to all the tourists. When describing U.S. intervention, the video says, "And the Americans arrived like a crazy batch of devils."

Third are the jungles. In less than a two-hour drive from HCMC, you can be in the Mekong Delta. Jeff, Greg, my caregiver, Lisa, and I took a tiny riverboat through the Mekong Delta to Cambodia. The result was a truly unforgettable and spectacular day-long journey in the jungles of Vietnam. Just witnessing the floating markets in Vietnam is an absolute traveling *must see*. The markets consist of tons of tiny boats floating on the river, filled to the gills with the most incredible fruits and vegetables you've ever seen. The colors, smells, tastes, and cacophony of noises these markets create is more than enough to make up for the long flight to 'Nam (approximately eighteen hours nonstop from New York-JFK).

At Angkor Wat in Siem Reap, Cambodia, with attractive caregiver Lisa, Jeff, and Greg. Also not exactly a wheelchair accessible place. But we still effin' conquered it, baby!

Fourth is the opportunity to say, "Viet-Fucking-Nam, Man!" from *Forrest Gump* every chance you get. It never gets old.

Fifth are the beaches. I never made it to any of them, but I heard they're beautiful.

And finally, the big kicker: the prices and the people! The cost of everything is beyond reasonable, and the Vietnamese people are some of the nicest, friendliest, sweetest, most resourceful people I've ever met in all my travels (these people waste nothing). It could be they are nice to everyone, but my theory is that traveling there as an American is actually an advantage. Once they hear you're American, it's as if they then go out of their way to let you know they have no problem with you—even if Americans are a crazy batch of devils.

Welcome to the jungle . . . of Vietnam.

You must visit Vietnam!

&. TURKMENISTAN. (Small country in Central Asia bordered by Uzbekistan, Afghanistan, Iran, the Caspian Sea, and Kazakhstan.)

I'm not necessarily recommending you travel here, it's just that my experience in this country was so bizarre that it makes *my* top five. I traveled to Turkmenistan in 2005, when their president at the time was an absolute freak. No exaggeration. This psycho first renamed himself "Turkmenbashi" (which means "Chief of the Turkmen"), and then mandated the calendar be redone to change January to his new name, April to his mother's name, and September to the name of a book he wrote, called *Ruhnama*. He put pictures of himself on basically everything, including their currency, most every building, billboard, and light post, and had statutes of himself erected virtually everywhere.

In the center of Ashgabat, the capital city of Turkmenistan, there was a golden statue of Turkmenbashi with his arms outstretched, atop a 230-foot tower. The statue actually rotated to keep him always facing the sun. There was also a large statute of the world breaking into two, and a woman hoisting a golden child from the abyss—this to replicate his mother, who died in the 1948 earthquake when he was a baby, while he survived. And in two of the cities I visited, there were thirty-foot-tall replicas of *Ruhnama* that actually opened up at certain times of the day to play a short movie about (you guessed it) him on its giant pages.

Ashgabat is also home to one of the largest markets in the world. It's said you can buy anything there from a camel to a jeep, and all things in between. And while they do not openly advertise the selling of people, later that night when we went to a small hotel bar, our tour guide (required by the government to be with us at all times) told me in a thick Russian accent as we watched several women dancing on the dance floor, "Pick any one you like. I promise to get her for you at a good price." I declined.

It was at this market in Ashgabat where I experienced something to a level I never imagined. One thing I've learned from my

Oh, yes, this book opens!

travels is how the United States is head and shoulders above other countries regarding the acceptance of and the possibilities afforded to people with disabilities. In many countries, people in wheelchairs are seen as people simply in need of charity.

I was in Tbilisi, Georgia, the first time someone ever approached me to give me money. This individual saw me sitting in my wheelchair and just assumed I must be begging. Admittedly, I was extremely hungover at the time and sitting next to a goat tied to a post when this person approached me. But it still surprised me they viewed me as so downtrodden that I needed their handouts. Certainly they failed to notice I was sitting in a top-of-the-line manual wheelchair which cost me thousands of dollars, or that I was wearing designer prescription sunglasses which were equally as obnoxiously expensive.

In my many travels since then, I've unfortunately been offered money more times than I care to remember—although never to the extreme like at the market in Ashgabat. Most of the kiosks there were run by women, and as soon as I approached a kiosk to peruse whatever wares they were peddling, they'd instinctively dip into their pockets and try to hand me money. And when I declined their offers, they looked at me with obvious confusion.

At a train station in Tbilisi, Georgia, moments before being offered money as a beggar for the first time. (Might have been because of the ugly hat.)

Making my way down the aisles with this scenario playing itself out over and over, word of mouth eventually began to catch up to the other vendors. The woman at the prior kiosk would yell over to the next something which must have been like, "Hey, Nastya, that incredibly handsome, intelligent, and strapping young cripple boy isn't begging for money and he won't take it." (Or something to that effect.) And so it didn't take long before each vendor realized I wasn't there to receive money from them. Instead, while looking at me with astonishment and smiling, they realized I was actually there to buy things from them with my own money.

To be totally accurate, however, I should say that all the vendors except one had this realization. There was one extremely (bordering on freakishly) persistent woman who followed me throughout the day and would not take no for an answer. She just kept offering me her meager coin (worth a fraction of a penny). Eventually I acquiesced, but only if she agreed to take a picture with me. It remains the only money I've ever accepted as a beggar. (Despite my friends always begging *me* to take the free money!)

I could write about the oddities of Turkmenistan forever, including their laws against lip synching, or their required exercise regimens, or the massive mosque built in the middle of the desert with an entryway that read, "The Koran is Allah's book, *Ruhnama* is the holy book" (it takes some stones to include that over a mosque), or the façade of a central square in Ashgabat made of white marble buildings and countless fountains—a place where no one lived but which drained all the water from the surrounding cities.

At a market in Ashgabat, Turkmenistan, moments after accepting the first (and only) money I've ever accepted as a beggar. (Again, might have been the hat.)

Turkmenbashi died in 2007. I have no idea what that place is like now, but visiting there blew my mind.

ZIMBABWE. Besides the aforementioned close call with a crocodile, I also found myself within fifteen feet of a stampeding elephant while fishing on a riverbank, had the tusk of a different elephant come within ten feet of my head when it almost ran into our jeep, and damn near flipped over in my wheelchair while speeding away in a motorboat to escape from a deranged lion (all true, and thanks, Jeff, for catching my chair). But risk/reward, right?

Going on a truly legitimate safari is something everyone should experience in their lifetime. And by *truly legitimate,* I mean no other safari vehicles are around you, you sleep in a tent or a hut (I also safaried on Fothergill Island), and you see tons of active animals. (If you pet anything on your safari and still have your arm below your elbow, then you got ripped off.)

It's difficult for me to say for sure, however, whether now is a good time to visit Zimbabwe. Their president, Robert Mugabe, has

Preparing to board our tiny plane and fly "into the bush" at Mana Pools, Zimbabwe, with Greg and our pilot.

so thoroughly and royally shafted this country that you may not experience the same amazing trip I did in 2003. Nonetheless, I'll attempt to describe one scene to you, and then you decide whether visiting Zimbabwe sounds awesome:

You're lounging outside your tent on a lazy afternoon of pristine summer weather. There's not a single cloud in the cobalt blue sky. No humidity. No bugs. There's a slight breeze and glorious (although surprisingly gentle) sunshine. You then look up to watch the baboons playfully swing from the shadowy branches above you.

Next, you look to your left, where off in the distance you see a Cape buffalo wading through the golden, sunlit sage. Or is it a Cape buffalo? You aren't so sure. Its head and body look so thick and dark you wonder if it's really not the stump of a tree. After all, a perfectly picturesque baobab tree is right next to it. So you reach for the compact binoculars hanging around your neck, and only then you clearly see the matted-down horns on its flat head—a sight both real and completely prehistoric.

Beyond the Cape buffalo are several impala (deer) grazing. They're elegant and peaceful, but by now they serve as more of a background (read: you've already seen enough impalas to last you for the rest of the trip).

More to the front of you, but still slightly off to your left, are two elephants slowly making their way towards the Zambezi River. They are arresting and totally free.

The Zambezi River is directly in front of you—behind the trees with the baboons—and it's when you look at the river that you really want to pinch yourself. *Can this be real, or am I dreaming?* Because it's there, interwoven within the glistening ripples of the river, that you see several huge hippos bobbing in the water and standing on the riverbank. *Holy moly, those things are big. And what are those noises they're making?* (You'll end up wondering about those noises again later that night, as you lay awake in your tent and listen to them.) Equally baffling, however, is the fact that the hippos don't seem concerned at all by the six enormous crocodiles—each about twelve feet in length—sunning themselves on the same riverbank, only ten yards away.

Finally, as you look to your right, you see two of your best friends in the whole wide world, as well as a campsite, and something cooking over an open flame, even before you smell the amazing aroma of dinner.

It's an idyllic panoramic view that I will never forget. It was the most surreal and spectacular Garden of Eden scene, which transcended anything my imagination could ever attempt to muster. It made me feel alive with every fiber of my being. And it's a memory Greg, Jeff, and I have talked about more times than their poor wives care to remember.

  ♿ ISRAEL AND JORDAN. (More specifically: Jerusalem and Petra.)

If you travel to Israel, it is Jerusalem which is like no other city in the world. It is positively unparalleled. Once there, however, it would be a shame to miss seeing Bethlehem, Nazareth, Jericho, and the Dead Sea. (I wouldn't bother with Tel Aviv. There are more orthodox Jews walking around New York City than I saw in Tel Aviv. But I hear it has a pretty good night life.)

Reading and hearing about the Middle East peace crisis is complicated enough, but when you have no context to frame the problem, it's damn near impossible to get your arms around any part of it. You need to visit Israel to begin to grasp how intertwined the daily lives of Israelis and Palestinians are, to hear their stories firsthand, and to realize how deep their animosity for each other runs historically, while at the same time how shallow it is becoming.

I'm not a big fan of Facebook, but I heard several young Israelis and Palestinians repeat a similar line. I'd ask an under-twenty-five-year-old Israeli what he or she thought of the Palestinians, and they'd say, "They're a bunch of killers and can't be trusted. Then again, I have a few Palestinian friends on Facebook, and they're all right." And I'd receive the same reply in reverse when I asked young Palestinians the question.

So maybe there's hope.

When visiting Jerusalem, however, I found myself being skeptical of such hope. There, I marveled at how it ever works at all.

I can think of no better example of this than in the walled-off Old City of Jerusalem. Within these walls (and immediately outside several of its gates) is the most dramatic display of a tinderbox you'll ever see. It's a place seemingly ready to explode at a moment's notice. Jews, Christians, and Muslims basically live on top of each other there, and all are intimately connected to their own religious beliefs. All of them outwardly exhibit those beliefs, and all of them are intensely passionate that the ground beneath their feet is fundamental to their beliefs.

The fact that these collided worlds exist with only occasional bloodshed (at least in recent years) is nothing less than a symbiotic miracle. Watching throngs of orthodox Jews confidently process along HaNevi'im Street toward Damascus Gate, past the hardened eyes of chain-smoking, coffee-guzzling Arab taxi cab drivers is mind-boggling. Living with this intensity day after day is nearly impossible to fathom.

Yet for the casual traveler, there's an easy escape: go see Petra in Jordan!

At the Wailing Wall in Jerusalem, Israel.

Odds are that unless you're a Jewish school kid qualifying for several free trips to Israel, once you visit, you won't be back—so DO NOT miss going to Petra.

There are many ways to get to Petra from Jerusalem. My trip to Israel began in Lebanon. I then flew to Amman, Jordan (spent two nights there—it's an okay city) and hired a driver to Petra. Another common way to reach Petra is to rent a car in Jerusalem and drive to Eilat (an overpriced beach town with pretty good food and lively nightlife) and then cross the border at Eilat into Aquaba, Jordan. I spent one night in Aquaba because I figured it might be cool, and I mistakenly thought it was too late in the day to cross the border into Israel. The only highlight (or lowlight) of Aquaba was that I'd never seen women wearing burqas at the beach until trapped in that shithouse-mouse of a city for about sixteen hours. (Never visit this place!)

Once in Petra, I took one of the most painful horse-and-carriage rides of my entire life through its breathtaking desert valleys. But the pain in my bony booty has long since gone away, and what's left is a memory of one of the coolest things I've ever seen.

Google Petra (where *Indiana Jones and the Last Crusade* was filmed) and then start planning your trip to go see it. Then again, if the images of cities carved into the faces of stone don't intrigue you, then I suggest you continue traveling on your "foreign" vacations to all-inclusives in Cancun and Puerto Vallarta. It's obvious your version of being Indiana Jones includes an All-You-Can-Eat-Buffet and hardcore karaoke on the promenade deck. And don't let anyone tell you different: you look local in those florescent shorts, white tennis shoes, and Fanny Pack. And you're right: everyone understands "American" if spoken slowly and loudly enough.

   ♿ RUSSIA. (More specifically: Moscow and Saint Petersburg.)

You know you've hit *Veteran Traveler* status—or *Spoiled Brat Annoying Snob* status) when traveling to Europe doesn't seem extremely exciting. Don't get me wrong, I'm not saying there aren't plenty of places in Europe I still hope to see. It's just that at this point, European traveling lacks the exotic element and challenge that really fires me up

That being said, for those who love the history and architecture of a European city, visiting Moscow and Saint Petersburg are very much European cities, but they're infinitely more exotic. Most travelers visit Paris and Rome, but Moscow and Saint Petersburg are less frequented.

Being in Red Square in Moscow one day, and then taking the night train and waking up in Saint Petersburg the next morning to see the Hermitage is fo shizzle off the hizzle, my nizzle! (Or if you're not yet fluent in Snoop Doggy Dogg (Lion) vernacular—it's pretty darn neato!) Even for those with limited vacation days, it's easy to see a lot in a short period of time by visiting Moscow and Saint Petersburg.

During my time in Russia, I also took the trans-Siberian train from Irkutsk to Moscow. The scenery out the window wasn't much different than in the U.S., though. I don't really recommend it, other than for the excitement of train travel.

Start prepping your liver now for this trip. You'll end up drinking plenty of vodka in Russia, but you'll never forget the experience.

♿ INDIA AND SRI LANKA.

I've never traveled to either one of these countries, but I hear amazing tales of them from my fellow journeymen.

I will eventually travel to both. I promise you that.

Never stop dreaming of your next big trip!

Back in the U.S.S.R.—Rockin' it in Moscow, Russia.

Chapter Fifteen

Travel Tips

TO DO BEFORE LEAVING:

♿ Purchase medical evacuation insurance. You do not want to be stuck in a foreign country sick or injured. Besides, this insurance is very inexpensive.

♿ About ten days before leaving, call bank (for ATM access) and credit card company. Let them know when you're leaving, when you're returning, and what countries you'll be visiting.

♿ Send yourself an email with scanned pictures of the front and back of your credit cards, ATM card, passport info, and important phone numbers.

♿ Visit your doctor to obtain antibiotics, shots, malaria pills, or whatever else you may need.

♿ If traveling in a wheelchair, confirm hotel availability first. (Do this first because once they hear you're in a wheelchair, they may say they're full to avoid hassling with it). Next, ask how many steps to enter, the width of their elevator door, and the dimensions of the elevator. Know the measurements of your wheelchair (length and width) in inches and centimeters.

♿ Visit the bank and withdraw lots of extra cash to use in case of emergency, to use when haggling (sometimes throwing in U.S. dollars can help) and for tipping (small bills).

♿ Order electric plug adapter(s) for the country/region (Amazon.com has plenty).

To pack:

- ♿ Passport
- ♿ Driver's license
- ♿ Credit card and back-up credit card
- ♿ ATM card
- ♿ Regular insurance card
- ♿ Medevac insurance card
- ♿ Extra cash (big and small bills—this may end up being the only money for days when/if things go wrong—make sure to bring enough)
- ♿ Rain jacket
- ♿ Hand sanitizer
- ♿ Hat with rim to block sun
- ♿ Sunglasses
- ♿ Shampoo and bar soap
- ♿ Watch (smartphone is okay, but a real watch is easier to check)
- ♿ Roll of toilet paper
- ♿ Sunblock
- ♿ Granola bars (these may safe your life)
- ♿ Gum/Breathmints (these may save someone else's life)
- ♿ Bug spray
- ♿ Good book to read (not hardcover)
- ♿ Joke book (these are awesome to pass time with groups)
- ♿ Phrase book of local language. Memorize how to say:
  - "Hello"
  - "Thank you"
  - "Excuse me"
  - "Good morning"
  - "You're beautiful"

 ♿ Travel Guide (I still think *Lonely Planet* does it best)

 ♿ Small pad of paper (Moleskine at a bookstore) and a good pen. Taking notes on a smartphone is not good enough. Often you'll need to have someone else write directions or recommendations in it, or rip out a page to give to a taxi driver.

 ♿ Medications (carry-on one bag with several days' supply and anything you need for the flight. Do not check *really* important meds in case bags are lost). The obvious meds to pack include:
  • Prescription medications
  • Tums
  • Tylenol, ibuprofen, and aspirin (take one aspirin on long flights to protect against blood clots)
  • Pepto-Bismol tablets (and liquid if possible)
  • Alka-Seltzer tablets
  • Imodium pills
  • Daytime and nighttime cold medicine
  • Band-Aids
  • Antibiotics
  • Antibiotic ointment

 ♿ Calculator (you'll need this at a market if you don't speak the language. Here's how you negotiate/barter: you show them the price you want, then they'll take your calculator and show you the price they want. Make sure you know the exchange rate both from U.S to local currency and from local currency to U.S. Often you get a better price when you use local currency. And even though smartphones have calculators, you do not want to hand it to everyone when negotiating)

 ♿ Camera (you may want something better than a smartphone)

 ♿ Alarm clock (smartphone is good)

 ♿ Charger cords and electric plug adapter(s)

 ♿ Duct tape (it'll fix anything, and tape down any liquid that can open)

 ♿ Lots of one-gallon zip-lock storage bags (pack anything that can leak in these, and you'll need them for wet clothes, gifts, things that must be kept dry, and whatnot.)

   iPod for music (smartphone is good)

   Secret money/passport holder (carry your emergency cash, back-up credit card, and passport in a hidden pouch. I wear one around my neck, under my shirt)

   Purse/man-purse/small backpack (you need to carry many of the above items with you each day while you're out exploring)

TO DO WHEN TRAVELING:

   Always negotiate the price *before* getting into any taxi cab.

   Always ask the price *before* ordering any food.

   Remember that haggling is a way of life in many other countries.

   Always grab a business card from the front desk when leaving your hotel/hostel. You will get lost, and the directions/address/phone number on the card may be your only hope.

   Never expect a taxi cab driver to give you change—give exact amount (with tip) whenever possible.

   When looking for directions and recommendations, find a nice hotel and speak to the concierge for all your questions. If they ask, "Are you staying here?" simply say, "Not right now, but I'm returning with a group in a few months, and I'm here now doing the research. We are considering staying in this hotel as a group, though." It works every time.

   Always have directions and recommendations written out for you in both English and the local language, and, if possible, include the phone number for where you're going (the cab driver will use it when lost).

TO DO WHEN EATING OUT (if you don't speak the language):

   Ask for a menu in English.

   Look up the words "traditional meal" in your phrase book and ask for that.

  ♿ Stroll around the restaurant, find a meal that looks good, and then point it out to the waiter.

  ♿ Put your hands under their respective armpits, flap your elbows, and cluck a few times—it's international sign language for ordering chicken.

  ♿ Although tipping is not expected in many countries, rewarding people for hard work is something Americans do well. If the waiter/waitress does a good job, tip even if not expected to.

  ♿ Keep an open mind!

Tip #7
Embrace the Opportunity of Your Challenge

THIS MAY BE THE MOST IMPORTANT tip of the whole book. It consists of two parts, and both parts are equally true. They're basically two sides of the same coin. You may view one side as negative and the other as positive, but both sides exist, whether you like it or not. And as is the case with everything related to perspective, it comes down to deciding where you choose to focus.

Here's the first part: *Your family and friends love you, but you will weaken that love and they will avoid you over time if you are depressing and self-absorbed.*

(I suggest you read that again to let it sink in.)

Granted, that's likely not what you want to hear if you're currently facing one of life's challenges. And certainly no one likes getting kicked when they're already down. But that doesn't make it any less true—even if it stings a little bit.

Sorry, dude!

F. Scott Fitzgerald, a Minnesota native who died at the tender age of forty-four after battling a lifetime of various illnesses, nailed this very point way back in 1925. Nick Carraway, the narrator of Fitzgerald's *The Great Gatsby*, said, "Human sympathy has its limits." And guess what? That's as true today as it was in the Roaring Twenties.

You need to recognize that there are limits to the sympathy you'll receive for whatever difficulty you're facing. Your family and friends will be there for you because they love you. But there are breaking points.

They'll support you, comfort you, hold you, and do anything they can to help you. They'll pray for you and with you. Your difficult time will be a difficult time for them—and this fact alone should lead you to believe that what's written above is true.

As long as you're miserable, those who spend time with you and care about you will be miserable, too. And normal people don't seek misery. Rather, they seek to avoid it. You know this is true. No one wants to be around someone constantly feeling sorry for themselves. It's depressing. It's not fun. It's sad. It's a total Debbie Downer.

So if your family and friends are normal people (which for your sake, I hope they are) then their natural inclination is to eventually avoid miserable situations. Their sympathy has limits.

But there's an upside to this: *Your family and friends love you, and you will strengthen that love and they will gravitate more towards you if you are courageous and handle your challenge with grace.*

(Repeat that to yourself, too.)

It's funny how in life we'll often do things for those we love that we wouldn't do for ourselves. On the surface, these acts may seem like unselfish acts, and it makes us feel better when we believe that's totally true. True love, it is often said, is the only unselfish emotion. But consider for a minute whether the contrary is actually more accurate, or at least equally accurate: that love (any form of love) is a selfish emotion.

It sounds counterintuitive—love is selfish—and I'll grant you that explaining this theory to your significant other on Valentine's Day will blow your chances of getting laid that night. But if you really think about it, an overriding reason (or at least an underlying reason) why we do things for those we love is because we want them to love us.

Be honest, when a friend calls and says they need help moving into their new apartment this weekend, you'll do it because you enjoy having them as a friend. You do it because you hope (or know) they'd do the same for you. You want them to consider you a good friend. You want them in your life.

This same logic applies to family, spouses, lovers, and others. You do for them because you want them to love you. It's an unromantic and highly cynical way to think about it, but it's true—at least to a certain extent. And my point in beating this theory to death is to highlight the wonderful opportunity that the challenge you're facing is providing you.

If you want those who love you to love you even more, all you have to do is choose to handle your challenge with courage and grace.

It's that simple and that difficult.

If you do this, I absolutely guarantee your family and friends will gravitate toward you and you will strengthen the love they have for you. They'll tell you how proud they are of you. They'll tell you they don't think they could handle the challenge you're facing as well as you are. They'll talk about you behind your back to other people, explaining to them how well you're facing this difficult situation. "My friend is amazing," they'll tell their other friends. "My child is incredible," proud parents will tell anyone who'll listen (and this time such pride will truly be warranted).

You'll inspire those who love you, and they'll want to be closer to you because of how thrilled and honored they'll be to have someone as special as you in their lives. Your positivity and strength will act as a magnet and will draw them in closer, and they'll love you even more.

All of this will naturally make you immensely proud. And your strength to continue to battle this challenge will then be fueled by this pride, which will build off of itself and grow, and allow you to continue on this positive path with infinitely greater ease. You will quickly find yourself holding your head high as you weather this storm. And you will deservedly reap the benefits of your effort.

The bottom line is that you're going to face this challenge regardless. So why not make the most of it? The old cliché is true: "You cannot choose the circumstances you face in life. You can only choose how to respond to those circumstances." It will absolutely feel wonderful to finally have power over a situation that likely left you feeling so powerless at first. You control how this challenge will impact you. You control how those around you will view your handling of this challenge.

You've been given an opportunity to make yourself and those around you very proud. It's certainly not an opportunity you wanted, but that doesn't change a damn thing. The simple truth is that you now have an opportunity to make the most of your challenge. So what are you gonna do?

Chapter Sixteen

New York

DESPITE MY RELATIONSHIP with Ann being a huge breakthrough in how I saw myself, I never dated anyone during my four years of living in Washington.

I went out to dinner a few times with a girl when I first moved to D.C. She was a physical therapist at National Rehab Hospital. We were about the same age and both single. During our first dinner together (which came about casually), a thought suddenly dawned on me: *Am I out on a date right now?*

Unfortunately, I made the ill-considered and ill-timed decision to verbalize my thought to her, which, rather predictably, then led to a very awkward discussion, including me blathering on about how I hadn't dated anyone since being in a wheelchair (read: TMI). After that, we carried on somewhat of a charade of dating for a few weeks— all until we went to a bar one night for her birthday. She politely introduced me to her friends, and then left for the packed dance floor, where she spent the remainder of the evening grinding on some random dude she just met. I never saw her again.

About a year later, I attempted to give dating another shot with the friend of one of my caregivers. She was from the Czech Republic, had emerald green eyes, auburn hair, and an hourglass figure that would be the envy of most amusement park rollercoaster rides. We spent ample amounts of time together, countless hours on the phone, and (much to the chagrin of my caregiver/her friend) one enlightening overnight trip in Annapolis, Maryland, where I was certain we'd emerge as paramours.

Yet despite my best efforts, nothing substantial transpired through any of this. A few years later, shortly after I moved to New York, she came for a visit. We went out to dinner, consumed quite a bit of wine, and returned to my apartment. Sitting together in soft lighting, overlooking the sparkling water of the Hudson River from my Upper West Side high-rise, I asked her frankly if she could ever see herself dating me. She said she didn't think so. After pressuring her to be completely honest as to why, she stated that while it was fine being seen with me in public as friends, she would be embarrassed to be seen with me as lovers. (Lesson learned: be careful asking for complete honesty.)

My last year in Washington, I finally became brave and committed enough to dating again that I joined Match.com. A lot of my friends were having success with Internet dating (it being somewhat new at the time) so I thought I'd give it a whirl. The few "winks" and messages I received, however, were from women who did not—let's say—"catch my attention" (translation: beggars can still be choosers). And of the even fewer messages I sent out to women, I received zero responses, despite having done meticulous research to find them, and being certain each of them was my long lost soulmate.

But, oh, goodness, how that all changed in the Big Apple!

Shortly after arriving in NYC, my Match.com account blew up with winks and messages. I couldn't believe the sheer volume and quality of my options.

My first date in New York was, in truth, my first real date *ever* since landing in a wheelchair—almost sixteen years after being injured. That's right: *sixteen years* without a true first date! The few quasi-dates and dalliances I'd had with women since my injury were all the result of pre-injury relationships, friends, too much tequila, or a combination thereof (which included Ann).

I arrived in Gotham at the spry, young age of thirty-five years old. Luckily, being in your thirties and unmarried in New York is more the norm than the exception. Within my first few weeks, I received a message on Match.com from a very impressive thirty-year-old woman, and as the *Magic 8 Ball* would say, "Outlook good."

She was stunningly gorgeous in the pictures she included online, a college graduate, and was making good money working as an events planner for a major Wall Street investment bank. We spent several weeks getting to know each other by trading messages and trying to schedule a date within our busy schedules, when, finally, a night appeared to work for both us.

"Tonight will work for me," I messaged her.

"And for me too :-)" she quickly responded.

I picked a chic bar close to my office that had both inside and outside seating. The plan was to meet at 8:00 p.m., although I arrived around 7:30 to secure a nice table in the outside/alley section.

Time clipped by slowly: 7:45, 7:55, 8:05, 8:15, 8:20. I sat at the table alone, nervous as hell, and with each minute that passed, I started to read, "Reply hazy; try again," and "Outlook not so good."

Did she chicken out? Did she walk in and see me in a wheelchair and leave? My mind was racing.

Of course I busied myself on my BlackBerry. I was a hotshot Wall Street lawyer, after all. So I pretended I was working—staring pensively and pathetically at a blank screen, pressing random buttons, and scrolling around to nothing.

Eventually I went inside to see if perhaps she was sitting in there; maybe there was some confusion as to where to find me. No luck. She wasn't there.

Pushing open the door to head back to my table, however, it seemed like the woman from the Internet pictures might have just passed by me at the same time. I sat at my outside table for a few minutes debating it in my mind, and then became convinced. I headed back inside at 8:25 p.m.

And there she was, sitting on a couch, feverishly typing on her BlackBerry as I approached. It was my date. I was certain of it. And she was beautiful.

"Rachel?" I asked with a broad smile, acting like I wasn't sure.

"Bob?" she responded, looking up at me without a smile.

Her look was of genuine confusion. She was an events planner on Wall Street, not a Broadway actress. So it took me all of about one second to realize that her countenance and the inflection in her voice were not the result of great acting—she was sincere. (If you're looking for someone in a wheelchair, I'm pretty easy to pick out.)

My heart sank.

"I have a table outside if you want to grab a drink," I said, barely able to breathe.

She rose from the couch looking like she'd just been punched in the stomach. What had happened was obvious, but I still had no idea how to handle it. There were two photos of me on my Match site that clearly showed me in a wheelchair. But women are often less superficial than men—and sometimes overlook these things, whether consciously or subconsciously.

Unfortunately, as hard as it may be to fathom, when we got to our table I actually managed to make everything one hundred times worse. She and I had exchanged many messages over the last few weeks, and she had asked me tons of questions about my recent trip to Central Asia. It was obvious she thought the trip was quite cool. So for some reason—in a very bizarre and terribly timed attempt at humor—when we sat down at the table I said, "I have to be honest with you, I made up that whole thing about traveling to ten countries last summer. I just use that story to help me get women."

The look on her face was of sheer horror!

When the waiter arrived, she couldn't even order. I had a glass of white wine in front of me, and she just pointed to it and said, "Yes, I'll have the same."

I tried to backtrack from the Central Asia "joke," but how do you convince someone a trip really happened? She was a deer in headlights, and I was the remnants of a deer already smashed against the grill.

I viewed the whole situation as a terrible case of Catch-22: if I asked if she'd known I was in a wheelchair from my pictures on Match, she would say, "Oh, yes, I saw the pictures, and it's no big deal," in which case it would be obvious she was lying. Or if I told her, "It's okay, you clearly didn't notice from my pictures that I'm in a wheelchair," she would likely respond by saying, "You're right, I didn't notice. But it's fine with me." And any fool could see it was anything *but* fine with her.

So instead of addressing the elephant in the room, we just sat there pretending we were having a conversation for a good five to eight minutes as I watched her unravel before my eyes. It was like I could actually see her mind spinning. She thought if she didn't get out of this "date" soon, she'd for sure be seen with me by her Wall Street cadre and they'd label her a "Timothy Cratchit Lover." Or she'd be stuck with me forever—and there was no way in hell that was going to happen to her.

So after the waiter returned with her wine, she feigned a few sips and then said she needed to go.

"I'm sorry, but I need to get up early tomorrow," she mendaciously announced, yet again failing to secure a Tony Award.

I tried my best to be a gentleman. I called the waiter over and asked for the bill. When he returned, I had every intention to pay it. I pulled out my wallet, but my nerves and crippled hands decided that now would be a wonderful opportunity to play a cruel joke on me.

I parted my wallet, spied a couple of twenties begging to be released, and reached for them—all the while remaining engaged in our make-believe conversation. As I went to remove the bills, however, the entire contents of my wallet started to fall out at once. *Don't panic,* I thought, acting as though I expected this to happen. I casually stuffed everything back in and started over—this time focusing a bit more intently. With a quick glance down and then straining to use every bit of my peripheral vision, I noticed a lone twenty had strayed from the pack and looked vulnerable. It wasn't quite enough to cover the bill, but it was a good start, so I ever so suavely glided my hand over it and pulled out a crisp ten dollar bill—less than half of what was needed. And she saw it, too.

Holy shit! She thinks I'm only paying half! Quick, put it back!

I spastically stuffed the ten back in and then, our of sheer desperation, thrust my entire balled-up fist into my wallet, hoping beyond hope to fish out that elusive freakin' twenty, which was now laughing at me. *Please give me that twenty! Or I'm happy with two tens! Four fives! Whatever! But hurry!*

And with that, out came a five and three raggedy-ass ones.

Son-of-a-bitch!

Just then Rachel leaned over to grab her purse in a fit of frustration. I think in her mind it was bad enough that everyone in the world now thought she wanted to bang Stephen Hawking, but being forced to watch me pathetically attempt to pay the bill was just too much for her. She'd had enough of this humiliation.

With my back against the wall, I was faced with no other choice: I simply turned over my wallet and let every bill fall into my lap. As Rachel quickly pulled her wallet from her purse in a disgusting display of egomania, insensitivity, and insecurity, I grabbed a twenty and a five from the pile.

"We're good," I said, handing it to our waiter. "Thanks so much." The waiter just stood there for a second, not exactly sure what he'd just witnessed.

Rachel quickly gathered her things as I stuffed bills back into my wallet. We then pushed back from the table and began our romantic stroll together out of the alley, toward the street. The walk consisted of no more than twenty feet, although I believe it was shortly before the tenth foot of my fairytale first date when Rachel raised her elegant hand high in the air. I wish I was kidding with this part of the story, but no. We honestly still had about ten feet of alley to walk before hitting the sidewalk, and Rachel had already assumed the position to hail a cab.

Once at the street, a cab arrived almost instantly. Rachel jumped in and had her phone to her ear within seconds. As she drove away, I felt quite confident I knew exactly what she was saying to the person on the other end of the phone. It didn't feel good, to say the least.

Later that night, I sent her a message to apologize (not exactly sure what for) and to address the elephant. I pointed out I did have two pictures on Match showing I was in a wheelchair, but said it was no big deal if she wasn't interested in dating. I was new in town, anyway, and she'd lived there for many years, so I told her I'd be happy just being friends. Perhaps she could show me around a bit, or I could join her for a happy hour sometime.

She never responded.

IN MY FIRST FEW WEEKS as a Wall Street lawyer, three separate events happened that stopped me in my tracks and left me with only one thought: *Are you effing kidding me?*

The first incident happened right away. I'd been staffed on several deals where companies were offering their stock to the public. None

Pimpin' as a Wall Street lawyer.

of these were the initial public offering for the company, so the stakes weren't nearly as high as they could be. As I toiled away one night in the office, a more senior lawyer, Amy, called me from "The Printer." Without wanting to bore you to death, The Printer is a place where the document used to sell stocks and bonds is finalized, printed, and shipped out to those who buy the security or are thinking about buying it. This document is called a "prospectus," and gallons of blood, sweat, and tears go into finalizing this seldom-read and hardly readable document.

Amy called me around 8:00 p.m. to ask if I'd be coming down to The Printer that night.

"I'm not sure," I said. "I'd like to see what it's like there, but I'm putting out a few fires right now on my other deals."

Around 9:30 p.m. she called back. She was still at The Printer, which was located downtown by Battery Park (the bottom tip of Manhattan), whereas I was in midtown, at Clifford Chance's office on West Fifty-Second Street by Sixth Avenue. (No New Yorker has ever said, "Avenue of the Americas.") She again asked politely and casually if I'd be heading down there sometime soon.

Still overwhelmed with all I needed to get done that night, but not yet willing to say no, I again told her I wasn't sure. "Let's see how it goes," I responded, trying to play it cool, like I might still pop by and see her around midnight on my way out to the dance clubs. When I worked at Arthur Andersen, I thought I worked pretty hard at certain times. During the tax season, I often worked twelve- to fourteen-hour days for months at a time, without a single day off. But here I was, still in the office as it was moving close to my fifteenth hour of the day, and there was no end in sight.

Around 11:30 p.m. Amy called once more. At this point, however, I knew there was no way I was going to meet her at The Printer. Besides, I felt pretty sure she was calling to say, "Never mind. Don't bother coming down. We're leaving now anyway."

Instead, astonishingly, Amy asked me once again if I'd be coming down to The Printer that night.

"Look, Amy," I finally answered with a growing sense of realism. "I'll be lucky if I get out of here in an hour or two, in which case I'm gonna head home."

After a long pause, Amy replied, "Well, okay," clearly surprised at my response. "But someone has to stay here all night long."

What? All night long? How can that be? And never sleep?

(Oh, and did I fail to mention Amy was about eight months pregnant at the time?)

Are you effing kidding me?

I couldn't believe people really worked this hard.

The second track-stopping event didn't affect me directly, but it left me with the same question nonetheless. We'd been drafting a contract all day (an underwriting agreement), and it was now late at night. The partner emailed me his comments and then called to say, "Why don't you drop these comments off in Document Production. Have them work on it tonight, and you can pick it up in the morning."

"What? What's Document Production?" I stammered.

"It's two floors up," he responded, half amused and half thinking I should already know this. "There's a room full of people who work on documents. It's staffed twenty-four hours a day, seven days a week. Just drop off these comments, and they'll have it ready for you by the time you arrive in the morning."

Are you effing kidding me?

The last occasion was by far the best. By then I felt like I'd seen it all. The phone rang one afternoon and a very senior partner was on the line.

"Can you be in Brazil this week?" Sara asked me directly but nonchalantly.

Trying my best to pretend like I received calls of this nature all the time, I responded, "It's Thursday, what do you mean by 'this week'?"

"Okay," she retorted. "Next week is fine, but we need to get to work tonight on drafting their prospectus." (Eleven years had passed since my interview at Arthur Andersen. It was now a foregone conclusion that someone in a wheelchair could fly.)

I quickly expensed two tickets to Sao Paulo, Brazil. One for me and one for my caregiver—the tickets were $7,000 apiece.

Are you effing kidding me?

A few months later, I was on the floor of the New York Stock Exchange. We'd helped the Brazilian airline, TAM Airlines, with their initial public offering and they were on the NYSE balcony ringing the opening bell. As I looked up and watched them smiling from ear to ear and shaking hands, it didn't seem they minded my $14,000 in plane fare. Then again, we'd just helped them raise $780 million.

Not much surprised me after that.

I DATED SEVERAL WOMEN in New York after my memorable first date with Rachel, and I met all of them on Match.com. One of these women was an extremely open-minded lass who I dated for about three months, and she seemed to care less about whether or not I was in a wheelchair. Unfortunately, it was a discovery in the bedroom that led to our break-up.

While engaging in some tantric reindeer games one night, she halted our activities by saying, "I have something to tell you that I should have told you a long time ago." Well, I'm not sure if anything good has ever followed a statement like that, but my hope of her telling me she was a multimillionaire did not happen.

"I know I told you I was separated from my husband," she began. (She said on Match.com that she was single, but on our first date she admitted she was actually separated and the divorce was almost final.) "But we're actually still married and we haven't filed any divorce papers yet."

Oh, goodness, I thought, and broke up with her not long after that.

The next woman I dated told me much sooner than the first that she'd initially lied about being single. That's right: it happened to me twice, back to back. Two women lied on their Match profiles about being single, and then lied to my face about the status of their divorce. (Be careful on these websites!)

I also believe some of the women I dated in New York (not all, but some) likely pursued me and were happier about dating me largely because I had enough money to make dating in New York fun.

Dating in any city is expensive, but dating in New York—going to nice restaurants, Broadway plays, and that sort of thing—is expensive as all get-out. The irony of living in Manhattan is that because it's so expensive, you need plenty of money to really be able to enjoy it. And unless you're a trust-fund baby, you're stuck working to make that money. And any job that pays you enough money so you're really able to enjoy the city also requires you to work so dang hard that you barely have time to enjoy it. So damned if you do and damned if you don't.

But I never had a real problem with those women who seemed attracted to me in part because of my financial success. The way I thought about it, having money was simply something that helped give me an edge over other guys, and why would I ever give that up? I'd worked hard and was still working hard to be where I was, and I felt like whatever fruits fell from the tree of success I helped grow, I had earned. Besides, I also wasn't going to pretend I had no money and sit around in the dark eating Ramen noodles with my dates just to see how much they really liked me just *for me*. Not to mention the fact I liked going to nice restaurants and Broadway plays, too. And let's be honest, it wasn't like I was making Donald Trump-size money. The women who thought it was cool I had a little bit of money would've dropped me in a New York minute (cliché works well there) if they weren't attracted to me for other reasons.

Yet even though I enjoyed making a decent amount of money, after working at Clifford Chance for a little over two years, I began to realize I didn't want to endure these brutal hours forever. Some nights I'd get one hour of sleep, some nights no sleep at all. Many people on Wall Street regularly go a night or two a week without sleeping. Jay, my favorite partner at Clifford Chance, told me he once went five nights without sleeping. I'm not sure at what point you start going insane without sleep, but it's got to be somewhere in the five-day range. Nora Ephron, the recently deceased essayist, novelist, screenwriter, and director who hailed from and lived in New York City, perhaps said it best when she said, "Insane people are always sure that they are fine. It is only the sane people who are willing to admit that they are crazy."

Well, I'm quite comfortable admitting I'm a little crazy. But after my first inpatient hospitalization since leaving Atlanta, I also knew my body couldn't take this beating much longer. My feet had become so swollen from a lack of sufficient hours in the bed that I eventually got an infection. Of course I ignored it, feeling I was "too busy," which landed me in the emergency room, followed by several days in the hospital on intravenous antibiotics, where I found myself trying to dissuade Mark, the Master Plumber, from blowing his brains out.

My worst day on Wall Street happened on one of my most intense days there. Several of the deals I was staffed on seemed simultaneously on the verge of exploding. I was the senior lawyer on one of these deals, and the junior lawyer totally flaked out on me. She knew she was quitting within a few weeks and started blowing off things she needed to do. By the time I realized what she was doing (or not doing), the whole deal was teetering on the abyss. My stomach was in such knots it eventually let loose.

Oh shit, indeed.

It was late winter/early spring, and the weather gods were smiling down upon me with the threat of a major snowstorm. Sequestered away in my office, I used the snowstorm as an excuse. I picked up the phone and called the partner in his office, which was only a few feet away from me. I told him I needed to leave right then to beat the snow, but I would keep working from home. It doesn't get much worse than this, but we were under the gun so intensely that by the time I got home I still had to sit there (in it) and work for several hours to beat our deadline. Luckily, years earlier, the Juder helped me realize that you can't quit just because it gets a little tough . . . or a lot disgusting.

I ultimately left Clifford Chance after about two and a half years. I would have stayed longer, even though the hours were wearing me down, but another law firm offered me a position which seemed too good to be true. Jay and the other partners tried to convince me to stay, and even offered me other positions at Clifford Chance which required fewer hours (and paid a little less money), but my mind was made up. Besides, every place I'd worked in my career had been a tremendous experience. I was certain the next place would be more of the same.

I was also certain I was head over heels in love with New York City. My family and friends still periodically asked me about The Ten-Year Plan (returning to Saint Ben's/Saint John's to teach), but we were only in year seven. So I started at a new law firm and bought a one-bedroom condo on the Upper West Side, one block away from Central Park (Fifty-Eighth between Eighth and Ninth). All-in after remodeling, I paid close to three-quarters of a million dollars for a little over six hundred square feet. (Alas, the pre-bubble housing market.)

I was living alone for the first time in my life—a feeling of spectacular independence known to everyone who has had the privilege of experiencing it, and a feeling magnified a trillion times over if you're someone who thought you'd *never* be able to experience it. I also rented a studio apartment in the same building for my caregiver (an additional $2,500 a month expense), so with mortgage, maintenance, and rent, I was paying over $6,000 a month just on housing.

I was absolutely living a dream. Every day I went to work through the electric streets of the city, I felt I needed to pinch myself. I was thrilled to be part of such an incredible scene. It's nearly impossible to stroll the streets of New York without regularly shaking your head and thinking, "Only in New York." The cast of characters and settings is everything it's portrayed as and more. I remember the first time I visited New York, two words kept running through my mind: no hype. Everything I'd seen, read, or heard about the city that never sleeps was all true—none of it was hype. And after about a year of owning an apartment and feeling like a "true New Yorker," it all completely fell to hell in a hand basket.

The job with the new law firm was a debacle from start to finish. I wasn't getting much work, and the work I was getting wasn't what I'd been told I would be doing. After a year of working there, it was clear there was no way this job was going to last. I came home from work one day when the Juder was visiting me in New York and told her I was applying to Saint Ben's/Saint John's. Almost eight years had passed since I had graduated from law school, and despite how much I loved New York, if I was serious about actually going back, I felt now was the time to put up or shut up.

I had been watching the job postings at Saint Ben's/Saint John's on the Internet for years, and fortunately a position was currently available. I hurriedly put together an application and fired it off. A few months later, I received a phone call with their decision: "Sorry, but we have a hiring freeze right now. We're not hiring anyone for next year." It was early 2009, and the housing and stock market crash were causing the world to hang on the cliff of financial ruin. Everyone was freaking out, including CSB/SJU.

And so I sat in New York at this train wreck of a job debating whether I really wanted to return to Collegeville and why. I knew if I left New York in the immediate future I'd take a thumping on the sale of my new apartment. I contemplated whether I should first try to work in a different department of my current law firm, apply to other firms, or try to go back to Clifford Chance. But was that what I really wanted?

The more I thought about it, the more I realized that even though I loved living in New York, my life had largely become a pattern of extremely hard work, followed by family and friends visiting where I could afford to be very generous on the best restaurants, bars, and Broadway plays, followed by more hard work, followed by waiting for the next group to visit. It was definitely fun for a while, but the work itself held no meaning for me—much less, it seemed, to anyone else.

Returning to Washington was an option I also contemplated. I could have likely returned to the SEC, and I seriously considered heading back to Capitol Hill. In addition, as one of life's strange twists, my junior varsity high school football coach was Joe Scarborough, a guy who traded in his whistle and tight Sansabelt polyester shorts to become a Congressman for a while, and now was a major star in political television. Joe and I had remained friends all these years, and having friends in high places can often help.

But half a year passed as I pondered what I wanted to do with my life, and I never applied to any other jobs. Yet with each passing day, I

In Zoo York City on the set of MSNBC's *Morning Joe* with Pensacola friend Joe Scarborough, Mika Brzezinski, former NYC mayor Michael Bloomberg, and a group of Johnnies and Bennies.

became more and more certain that I knew *exactly* what I wanted to do—I just needed to find a way to make it happen.

Eventually the hiring freeze at Saint Ben's/Saint John's was lifted and a job posting popped up on their website. I quickly threw my chips on the table again. This time, however, I doubled down. I put my condo up for sale, hired a moving company, and shipped everything I owned to St. Cloud, Minnesota. My decision of where I was going to work had been made; being offered the job was just a matter of details.

As all this played out, I developed a plan to do something I'd always dreamed of doing: volunteering overseas. Other than the few times I'd been a peer counselor to individuals with a spinal cord injury, I'd basically done nothing to help people with disabilities. I realized that now was a wonderful window of opportunity to give back a little bit. I found an organization named Cross Cultural Solutions and decided they were perfect for me. Not only did they have options for volunteering in Central America (which is where I wanted to go), but they also offered health insurance.

I parted ways with my law firm and spent a few months in Pensacola with the Juder organizing my next adventure. I advertised on the Internet for a caregiver to travel with me for six months as I volunteered in Central America, and Craigslist came through yet again. Before I knew it, I was on a flight to Guatemala. My first stop was volunteering at an orphanage in Guatemala City for children with disabilities.

I was choosing once again to make my life exciting (and hopefully doing some good at the same time).

About two weeks before leaving, however, I received a phone call from CSB/SJU. They were granting me an opportunity to come to Collegeville and formally interview for the teaching position. My application had made it through several rounds of eliminations and I'd survived a phone interview. It was now down to me and one other candidate.

I flew to Minnesota from Pennsylvania the night before the interview. It was late December and I'd been spending Christmas in Newtown, Pennsylvania, with Karen, Matt, the kids, and the Juder. The caregiver helping me in Minnesota, Dan, a Johnnie, was an old friend who really only knew how to take care of me at night, so we were winging it the morning of my interview. (I considered staying up all night like I did with my interview at the SEC, but decided against it.) I wore a suit and tie for my interview, which began with breakfast at 7:00 a.m. in the school refectory (dining hall).

While interviewing with a female professor around 8:30 a.m., I looked down and noticed that Dan forgot to zip the fly of my pants—my barn door was wide open. With no breaks scheduled until lunch and maladroit hands, my only option was to lean forward and strategically position my tie.

Once at lunch and finally alone in a bathroom stall, I tried desperately to zip up my fly from every angle my Tiny Tim hands would turn, all before hitting that point of being in the bathroom an awkward amount of time. I'm sure if anyone noticed my fly was down earlier in the day, they felt confident I'd take care of it once I went to the restroom. When I returned with my fly still down, however, they must have wondered what in the hell was wrong with this weirdo.

In the end, I interviewed in front of about fifteen students and a handful of faculty, all the while knowing full well my fly was completely down. I mostly tried to stay behind a desk. But in the few instances when I was forced to move around, I was filled with fear that my tie would shift and expose a pink panther. And little did my audience know that as I presented before them, my life's possessions were already sitting in a warehouse a few miles away.

My buddy Greg drove up to Collegeville to pick me up after the interview and haul me back to the airport in Minneapolis. I think all you can really hope for in life is to have a few good friends who you can pull into a bathroom and say, "Hey, man, would you mind zipping my fly up?"

About two months later, an international phone call was placed from Collegeville, Minnesota, to Guatemala City, Guatemala. It was an offer for a tenure-track teaching position in the Accounting and Finance Department at the College of Saint Benedict/Saint John's University starting in the fall.

"I accept your offer," I said loudly and clearly, thrilled to my absolute core. I then laughed to myself, thinking about what I could have said: *I accept your offer. In fact, I accepted it about a year ago, if not closer to ten years ago.*

I was on my way to Collegeville . . . again!

Tip #8
It's Okay to Look

WHEN YOU'RE IMMERSED in a crowd of people speaking a foreign language, it's amazing how your ears can zero in on the sound of a few bits of English spoken amid the cacophony.

The sounds around me, however, were not only those of a foreign language (Spanish), but also of random cries, yells, yelps, whimpers, and the indecipherable language of children with profound mental and physical disabilities.

I was volunteering in an orphanage in Guatemala City where the children had basically been dropped off at birth. These children would live their entire lives here, venturing outside its walls only a select few times, if at all. They typically never saw their parents again, and any potential they may have had within themselves would likely never be realized.

The first day I was there, I arrived around 8:00 a.m. with my caregiver. We looked around to make sure it was all wheelchair accessible, and seeing that it was, I asked her to return at 12:30 p.m. to help push my manual wheelchair back to where we were staying.

Later that evening, Virginia, the woman running the volunteer program in Guatemala through Cross Cultural Solutions, received a call from the orphanage.

"Listen," they said to her in Spanish. "We have enough handicapped children to take care of. That man you sent here today cannot come back unless he brings his nurse with him. We are not going to be responsible for taking care of him, too."

My second day volunteering in Guatemala, therefore, I did not volunteer at all. I stayed home in protest, telling Virginia this was bull excrement.

"I don't need a nurse or caregiver with me all day," I exclaimed. "I only need help at night and in the morning. Besides, I have a cell phone if anything goes wrong. But I do not need her with me when I'm volunteering. I just came here from working on Wall Street, for Christ's sake! Don't you think I can handle this?"

Virginia was skeptical. She was a very educated and wise woman, but she admitted she hadn't had much exposure to people with disabilities. According to her, people in Guatemala generally coddled the disabled, keeping them at home and caring for them for life. The disabled did not work. And this was 2010, not 1950.

It took some convincing, but Virginia ultimately sided with me. She stood up to the people running the orphanage. We agreed to have my caregiver join me for a few more days, but it didn't take them long to realize I didn't need someone there to take care of me just because I was in a wheelchair.

Shortly thereafter, alone at the orphanage one day, I kept hearing English being spoken, somewhere, even though I knew no one there spoke English. It sounded like a recording but I couldn't make out the words. I could just hear it playing over and over.

I followed the sound through the maze of rooms until I found a young boy in a room watching a computer monitor as a YouTube clip replayed itself. The orphanage was unquestionably too poor to have Internet access. Instead, a very old computer must have been donated, and someone loaded this clip on the hard drive.

The boy watching this clip looked to be around twelve years old. He had obvious, severe muscular dystrophy. And although at first glance it looked inhumane, his arms and legs were literally tied down to his dilapidated wheelchair with old Ace bandages.

He couldn't speak at all (Spanish or English). He could only make grunting noises. When he saw me enter the room, however, he communicated naturally: he tilted his head slightly to one side, rolled his eyes toward the computer, and grunted to direct me to watch what he was watching.

It was when I neared the computer that my genuine confusion set in. In the clip the boy was watching, a crowd of young school girls listened intently to someone on a stage speaking English. The girls were wearing uniforms, so it appeared to be some sort of Catholic grade school presentation.

What caught me off guard was the person on stage. Astonishingly, he had just a head and a torso. That's it. No arms, no legs—just the head of a grown man and a small torso.

I sat there with this boy tied down to his wheelchair and watched this clip five or six times (it was only two minutes, forty-one seconds long). The name of the man on stage was Nick Vujicic. He's a motivational speaker from Australia, and he was born this way. Ironically, scrolling at the bottom of this particular clip were Mandarin and Spanish subtitles, but the boy watching for inspiration didn't know how to read. Not that his disease prevented him from learning, it was just no one had recognized his potential to learn or taken the time to teach him.

Watching this young man (it turned out he was actually twenty-four years old) stare at the computer screen and be inspired by someone with no arms and no legs reminded me that you never know who you're inspiring when you're facing one of life's challenges—and you should always keep your eyes open for others who can inspire you.

Too often we feel guilty about looking at that person who is so clearly facing a difficult challenge in his or her life. It somehow seems wrong to feel better about our own situation by comparing ourselves to them. Well, I'm here to give you full permission to do just that: go ahead and look. Look all you want.

Certainly you shouldn't stare. But it's important to remind yourself that things could always be worse. At a minimum, the challenge they're facing (and you're not) is one less thing for you to worry about.

I recently saw a wonderful example of this on the Internet. Abby and Brittany Hensel are conjoined twins, born and raised in Minnesota. They basically have one body and two heads. Now let me say this: I know what it feels like to have people stare at you. But I can't imagine what it's like for them. (And I'm not just talking about when they wear paraphernalia from Minnesota's professional baseball team.) That being said, they may look at me and feel thankful they can walk up and down stairs, use any public restroom they want, and be independent of caregivers.

I'm sure they have their good days and bad days (as we all do), but from what I can tell, they're just trying to live a normal life despite their challenges. They inspire me. The young man in Guatemala inspires me. Nick Vujicic inspires me. So many, many people living their lives on ventilators, with head injuries, serious depression, addiction, chronic debilitating pain, and countless other maladies inspire me. And I hope they don't mind if I'm able to draw strength to face my own challenges by watching them as they so courageously and gracefully face their own challenges.

In return, I'm very comfortable and quite proud if others are able to draw strength and perspective from watching how I face my challenges. Please look at me all you want.

Because it's when you finally become thankful for what you do have, rather than focusing on what you don't, that you can begin to embrace and enjoy the one life you've been given.

Chapter Seventeen

Collegeville 4.0

THE JUDER IS FOND of saying I became the man at nineteen or twenty years old she hoped I'd be at forty or fifty years old. And while few things in life are certain, considering the path I was on before my injury, there's no way in hell I would have ever ended up where I am today, or, in all likelihood, who I am today.

My injury forced me to think about goals and pursue them more doggedly than is typical of many young people. It also necessitated that I become a bit more serious and disciplined. Not that I didn't have (and continue to have) plenty of fun. But when a caregiver needs to put you to bed at a certain time, blowing off everything until midnight is not an option. Likewise, focusing on getting good grades and pursuing a career in a well-paying field also seemed infinitely more important given the need to financially support my medical care. (Digging ditches was no longer an option.) And by both choice and circumstance, time spent dating was not much of a distraction. I have few regrets in life, but I do regret not becoming more comfortable with myself sooner, and not having more faith in other people's ability to look past the superficial.

My injury also allowed me to become much closer with my family and realize how precious and important they are. Similarly, many of my friendships (several I had before my injury, and virtually all I've made since) are significantly more substantive and meaningful.

But I certainly didn't need to have my neck broken for my life to turn out this way. No one needs to become a quadriplegic before asking themselves the three questions I pondered in a garden in Atlanta:

Who do I want to be?

How do I want my family and friends to see me?
What kind of difference do I want to make with my life?

As I write this chapter, I'm forty-three years old and have been in a wheelchair for twenty-four years. I've undeniably made plenty of mistakes in my life. But overall, I'm proud of what I've accomplished thus far, the life I'm currently leading, and who I am. I have family and friends who are immensely proud of me, who love me dearly, and would quite literally lie down in traffic for me. (Or at least would consider it if the street were blocked off.) I've been a groomsman in several weddings. I was Jeff's best man (gave one hell of a speech). And I've had many people say incredible things about me to my face. More importantly, I often hear secondhand stories, where people have said amazing things about me behind my back.

When Father Cletus heard through the grapevine that I'd applied for a teaching position at CSB/SJU, he picked up the phone without any prompting and called the chair of my department. He minced no words in his recommendation: "You definitely should hire Bob." (And then added a few awkward comments about my past.) It's funny how life can often come full circle.

I ended up beating The Ten-Year Plan by one year: I started teaching at Saint Ben's/Saint John's nine years after graduating from law school. I now live in St. Cloud and miss New York City almost every day. I absolutely don't make a lot of money at my job. And I lost pretty much everything I made prior to working at CSB/SJU in one real estate transaction on the Upper West Side of Manhattan.

Yet each morning when I turn off Interstate 94, take a left, and start heading to Collegeville, I see the bell banner of the Abbey church rising above the pine trees. It reminds me to focus on what's important. And most days, driving in my car alone, I literally say out loud, "This is the best decision I ever made."

I truly love my life.

Tip #9
Never Quit!

TOWARD THE END of my third year of teaching at Saint Ben's/Saint John's, a colleague stopped by my office to ask a few questions about advertising for liver donors. Her twenty-year-old son was dying of a liver disease.

Alex had been diagnosed with this disease about a year earlier. A few months after his diagnosis, in an unimaginable case of a double whammy, he found out he also had testicular cancer. Through chemotherapy and determination, however, he was able to beat that cancer. He was now back to focusing solely on his liver disease, which entailed getting a liver transplant.

His mother, Michelle, was asking me these questions because back when Karen was fighting leukemia, I'd helped put together a few bone marrow drives in case she needed a donor.

Alex was being treated at the Mayo Clinic in Rochester, Minnesota. When I first moved to Minnesota as a freshman at CSB/SJU, an attractive Bennie told me she was from Rochester, "You know," she said, "where the Mayo Clinic is?"

"Is that where they make mayonnaise?" I responded, only half-kidding. (I obviously knew nothing about the Mayo Clinic.)

As Michelle described to me the process for finding out if someone is a good match to be a liver donor, she mentioned an 800 number to the Mayo Clinic where the initial screening began.

Why don't I call the number? I thought. *Who knows, maybe I'm a match.*

A few days later, I picked up the phone and called.

It began ordinarily enough, I suppose. They asked my name, date of birth, height, weight, how I knew the potential donee, whether I'd ever been a patient at the Mayo Clinic, and that sort of thing. After about five minutes of questions, the woman asked if it would be okay if she transferred me to someone else.

"Sure," I responded.

A few moments later, another woman picked up the phone who was clearly nervous. Her voice had a detectible quiver, and her first question was for me to clarify why I'd been an outpatient at Mayo Clinic sixteen years earlier.

"I'm a quadriplegic," I answered. "I was having some urological issues." I gave her a bit more detail, but the inflection in her voice had made an obvious change. Yet it was unclear to me exactly which way the change went: either she'd now become very sweet and empathetic due to better understanding the medical issues I'd faced in the past, or, instead, she sounded overly materialistic and somewhat patronizing.

Eventually, and with what seemed like a total lack of forethought to whatever protocol she was supposed to be following, she blurted out in resignation, "Look, I've been working here for ten years, and I've never had this situation before. I don't know how to handle it. I think I need to speak to the board in the morning and ask their opinion."

I was completely confused. I'd simply called an 800 number and given basic information, and now the woman on the other end of the phone was freaking out.

Trying my best to rein in the situation, I said, "Listen, I feel like you're getting a little ahead of yourself. Why don't you just tell me how to get a blood test to see if I'm even the same blood type as Alex?" (After all, I'd been through this with Karen twenty years earlier. *Wasn't getting a blood test the first step?* I thought.)

"The board meets first thing tomorrow morning," she said. "I'll call you after the meeting."

After hanging up the phone, I became more and more disturbed by my conversation with this woman. *Why was she so freaked out?* I questioned to myself. *Shouldn't they at least see if I'm a match before they start worrying about whether they'd let a quadriplegic donate?*

And that's when it dawned on me: *They asked if I was ever a patient at Mayo so they could look up my medical information. I met all the other criteria from the screening, and that woman was freaked out because the computer told her exactly what my blood type is. I was a match, and she knew it, too. Hole-lee shit!*

I don't think I slept a wink that night. Before I went to bed, I consulted with my good friend, the World Wide Web, and she told me that giving part of your liver to someone is a fairly major operation. My liver would fully recover, but it would likely be as many as six months before I'd be back to normal, and I shouldn't plan on working for three of those months. With summer around the corner and being that I was a college professor, I figured I could probably finagle the three months off from work if we timed it just right. But could my body handle the operation? I wasn't so sure.

As I lay awake in bed with my mind racing, the irony of the decision struck me: when I was nineteen years old, I seriously considered killing myself. And now, here I was, all these years later, with a chance to save the life of a twenty-year-old.

How much easier would my decision not to take my own life have been if I had known then what I know now? I pondered. What if someone had said to me, "Hey, Bob, if you decide not to kill yourself, you'll spend the next twenty or so years doing some pretty incredible stuff, and then you'll have a chance to save the life of a boy about your same age—how's that sound?"

A question like that makes the decision seem pretty easy. And to me, it's just another way of describing what having perspective is all about, and what I hope this book has helped to provide. It's certainly not always easy to realize it at the time, but when you're facing one of life's challenges, putting that challenge into perspective is as simple as focusing on the past, opening your eyes to what's in front of you right now, and embracing the future.

To the extent you've endured or witnessed a challenge in the past which seems more difficult than the one before you, you're quick to realize you can handle the obstacle at hand. In other instances, you need only to stop focusing on yourself for a second and behold the struggles of those around you. Or, finally, in those rare instances when the challenge before you seems uniquely difficult, you must allow for time to pass in order to gain the necessary perspective. In those situations, the future will provide the perspective needed to help you realize you can handle this challenge. And as is so often the case, it will also illuminate the unexpected and magnificent surprises which accompany it.

I've had family and friends endure painful divorces, suffer with a wide range of injuries and illnesses, and lose loved ones to cancer, car accidents, suicide, and other unspeakable tragedies. And in every instance—even in the excruciating event of the death of a young child—they will tell you that it gets easier with time.

Like learning to play a musical instrument, it may take some practice—some getting used to. But *everything* gets easier with time.

Everything!

THE WOMAN FROM THE MAYO CLINIC called the next morning. She told me the board met and decided it was too big of a risk to permit me to donate. She admitted I was a good match but said they wouldn't allow a quadriplegic to go any further in the process. They concluded that being able to move all four was required to move forward.

I was both disappointed and relieved. I believe I would have donated if given the opportunity. But I also realize you never know what can happen in the future. Maybe someday I will have a chance to save someone's life. Or in less dramatic terms, I'll almost certainly have a chance to make a difference in someone's life.

Who knows? Perhaps I just did.

Acknowledgements

I entrusted only two people to read a draft of this book prior to trying to get it published. I chose the right two. Their comments made this a much better book and their encouragement fueled my drive to carry forward. Thank you, Amy "Bird" Lustig and Janean Kleist. You are both truly amazing and talented people. (Amy is one of Karen's best friends and lives down the street from her. Janean is one of my colleagues at CSB/SJU.)

I knew I would ask Michael Jones to help me with the cover of this book before even beginning to write a chapter. And while I imagined I'd never be able to afford the fees he charges for his talent, I felt I needed to at least try. His response to my offer says everything about him: "There is no fee. Sorry, I don't do business with family." Thank you, Mike! You are family, indeed. (He's Karen's next-door neighbor.)

To the wonderful people at North Star Press of St. Cloud: Corinne, Seal, Anne, Jenny, Jack, and Curtis. I sent a query letter to them on a late Sunday afternoon. By 10:00 a.m. the next morning, they asked for a sample of the book. I sent them the first seventy-five pages an hour later. And less than two hours after that, they sent me a contract. Thank you for believing in this book, North Star Press!

Next, I began writing "A special shout out to . . ." but saying "shout out" is sooo yesterday. So I won't. Instead, much appreciation goes out to Anna Jonas in the CSB/SJU bookstore for being my personal marketing consultant, and to Emily Krump (a loyal Bennie) for being by personal book industry consultant.

Finally, I hope thanking my family, friends, caregivers, the CSB/SJU community, and the World Wide Web is not necessary; I'd like to think the book does that on its own. But thank you nonetheless!